Free To Be Myself

Free To Be Myself

Ann Warren

HODDER AND STOUGHTON
LONDON SYDNEY AUCKLAND TORONTO

British Library Cataloguing in Publication Data

Warren, Ann
    Free to be myself
    1. Christian life   2. Self-realization
    I. Title
    248.4   BV4501.2

    ISBN 0-340-39031-X

*Hodder and Stoughton Editorial Office: 47 Bedford Square, London
WC1B 3DP*

Contents

	Foreword	7
1	Do I Really Matter?	11
2	Selfishness or Self Discovery?	19
3	What Went Wrong?	27
4	Front-Room Christianity	37
5	Clearing out the Cellar	49
6	How Do We Find Our Real Identity?	63
7	Real-Life Love	71
8	Real-Life Fellowship	79
9	On the Bottom Rung	87
10	A Complete Ministry in the Church?	95
11	Freedom To Be Myself	101
	Useful Addresses	110

Foreword

Why this subject?

Wherever I go I meet with people who seem to lack any real sense of self worth or identity. Many of them live their lives struggling to present a brave face to the world, but actually feeling very alone and unwanted on the inside. Usually they have no one with whom they can share these deeper needs and feelings; no one with whom they can risk 'being themselves' in a relationship.

Over the years since I first trained as a pastoral counsellor, I think it is true to say that I have been asked to speak on this subject more than any other, and this in itself must give some clue as to how many people recognise that there is something wrong in this area of their lives.

Time and again I have watched fascinated as different people have started on the journey of finding their own God-given identity (not just a carbon copy of Mrs Jones next door) so that a completely new quality of life has begun to unfold.

Unfortunately, it seems that the subject is a difficult one for some Christians to grapple with. There is an unspoken feeling around that we should not really be focussing on our own needs and problems anyway. Owning up to these seems rather like letting the side down, or admitting that the gospel formula for our lives is not really working as it should.

After all, surely, some people would say, concern with

self-centred interests should long since have been put aside
in taking up our cross to follow Christ?

Again, having been taught that all our desires are
basically sinful, many of us have tended to throw out the
baby with the bathwater. Gifts that have been given to us
both to use and to enjoy have frequently ended up in the
same rubbish bin as genuinely sinful desires such as greed
and selfishness, and many seem unable to distinguish
between the two. The result is often a rather restricted and
colourless lifestyle where everything is narrowed down to
activities that are overtly and obviously Christian, thus
missing out on the 'perfect freedom' and very real colour
that God has given us in His world.

Jane is married to a well-known Christian worker who
spends much of his time with young people. When I first
met her she was desperately struggling to 'be' and act as
she felt she was supposed to, with drainpipe jeans, arty
clothes and all the appropriate jargon. But from my very
first encounter with her it was clear that this was not the
real Jane! Moreover she was far from happy or at peace in
the 'role' that she felt she was supposed to be playing. As
we talked about her rather narrow and restricted
childhood, various interests and talents began to emerge
that it seemed she felt quite guilty about, since they did not
fit with her stereotype image of what a Christian wife and
mother should be.

When I pointed out that these were none the less gifts
that God had clearly given her to use (talents that she had
effectively buried) her face almost visibly brightened with
excitement and interest. Then, as she began to realise that
she was of *value herself*, the unreal outer shell began to
crack and the roots of abundant life started to move out at
last!

Today barely two years later, Jane is a visibly different
person. Because she is 'herself' and knows that God loves
and values her, she is much more relaxed and at peace, and
more able to go out in love towards others, as well as to

her own husband and family. In the clothes that she herself has chosen, and the gifts that she is using and developing, she is actually *being* a real living witness to the love of God in the world around her.

Over the last ten years I have met and talked with a great many 'Janes'. They come in all shapes and sizes, men and women, young and old. And they have this one thing in common – that they have never understood the wonderful truth that God has *chosen* them as individuals, because He loves them, and because He wants them to be *themselves* as real living lights in the world around them.

Because they are usually rather unsure people who have not received much love or encouragement either from their own families or from the churches they attend, they are often dutifully and rather drearily going through the motions of their faith. Somehow, somewhere, the streams of living water are missing, but they are afraid to talk about this, or even to enquire how and where these might be found. If they have doubts and needs then they will hug these to themselves at all costs, for admitting to this would surely be seen as unacceptable. And so the rather pointless and boring lifestyle goes on ...

The way they walk, the way they look, and everything that goes to make up what psychiatrists call body language, shouts from the rooftops that they feel unloved and unfulfilled in themselves – and yet when these people are believing Christians, it seems the most tragic denial of the very freedom that Jesus came to bring.

Certainly they have understood the vital truths of eternal life and salvation, in that Christ died for them personally, but not, it seems, that this quality of abundant life begins *here and now*, following the route that He has chosen for them as individuals. Which brings me to my second reason for wanting to write this book.

A long time ago now I asked God to show me what in particular He wanted me as a writer to do. I was pointed to a verse in Isaiah where the prophet is told to go outside the camp and 'sit where they sit'. And quite honestly when I sat outside some of our churches and fellowships, looking in, it was a pretty uncomfortable experience.

Because I very firmly believe that Christianity is caught before it is taught, I had to ask myself what, if anything, outsiders could see in the lives of some of our churches that they would actually want to 'catch' or to share.

People going dutifully through the motions of their faith, but showing all the signs that the abundant life which they spoke and sang about was not a *reality* in their own experience, were hardly 'salt' and 'light' to those around them! If anything it seemed that some of them were a living denial rather than a living witness, however genuine their faith may have been.

In the early church Jerusalem was agog with the amazing realisation of 'how much these Christians love one another'. But if you are unsure of yourself or your own value, it is very difficult to go out in love to those around you. The love of God must really be allowed to *come in* before it can be given out. In some cases I saw that self-conscious evangelism which did not show itself first in genuine outgoing love, no strings attached, was often doing more harm than good in the world outside.

And so I come to this book. If in the writing of it I should tread on any sore places, or say things in a way that may be hurtful to my readers I can only apologise. But if we are going to grow as people and become the salt and light that we are meant to be in the community, we are going to have to start from a position of rock-solid reality.

It can be painful, but as I know only too well there is really nowhere else to start.

1

Do I Really Matter?

'Who am I?' is a question we are hearing more and more at the close of the twentieth century. Sometimes it rings out with strident music from the pop songs of the day, at others it whispers despairingly from the hopeless contemporary drama of late-night television. 'Who am I?' and 'What difference does it make if I am here or not?'

As we look around us it is hardly surprising. While so many people live out their days on huge featureless housing estates, attending the same gigantic schools as thousands of others, and shopping at some clinically impersonal supermarket, it is almost inevitable that they will end up feeling little more than tiny cogs in a vast wheel over whose progress they have no control.

Old people die alone in blocks of flats where nobody knows them and the news of their passing comes only when the milk bottles pile up outside the door.

Even in the universe mankind feels more and more insignificant in a whirling mass of planets quite literally light years beyond his comprehension. At the same time popular science, although out of date, is still telling us that we all 'just happened' – tiny specks of irrelevant dust that will soon disappear, without any meaning to our ever having been here.

Alvin Toffler in his second book *The Homeless Mind* comments with some justification that man from whom science seems to have removed all possibility of faith was truly alone in the universe. In his words, it is 'the hardest loneliness of all to bear'.

Professor Joad has recently described a human being as 'Fat enough for seven bars of soap, iron enough for one medium-sized nail, sugar enough for seven cups of tea, lime enough to whitewash one chicken coop, phosphorous enough to tip two thousand matches, magnesium enough for one dose of salts, potash enough to explode one toy crane, and sulphur enough to rid one dog of fleas . . .' This is the sort of analysis guaranteed to make us all feel utterly and completely worthless.

How we cope

Is it any wonder then that people struggle to give their lives some transitory meaning – some colour, some identity, some difference at least from their fellow human beings?

If we do not actually resort to dyeing our hair in brilliant shades of pink or green, or spiking it all over our heads so that no one can fail to notice us, then there are plenty of other courses open to us – bigger and better cars, elaborate lace curtains in our windows, the very latest in fashion gear, or even struggling to gain the world record for yet another far-out activity that probably has no meaning or usefulness in itself, but will at least get us 'noticed' somehow.

Alternatively we may struggle to conform at all costs with the majority around us, so that at least we will feel included – one of the group.

Of course these are all fairly superficial things and relatively harmless in themselves, but they represent a much deeper hunger. Each one of us needs to know that we really matter to someone, that we 'belong' and above all that our lives have a meaning and a purpose.

Once upon a time our ancestors lived their lives in small villages where everyone knew everyone else, and families were on hand to give daily love and support. Today we are scattered across the country and across the globe. Newlyweds, if they are lucky enough to get a house at all, may settle in tiny terraced houses that are miles away from family and friends, and where most of the people around them are too busy in their own little boxes to have time to care about anyone else.

I believe that there are many people asking this question 'Do I really matter?' A line towards the end of the film of *Dr Zhivago* says it all, as the heroine disappears into the crowd for ever: 'She died a nameless number on a file long since mislaid.'

Does God really care?

Anyone who has come into a real encounter with the living God knows that there is a great deal more to life than all this represents.

While the science of the sixties was busy moving away from all possibility of a Creator God, well over half of contemporary physicists now acknowledge that there is no possibility of the world having come into existence 'by accident'. To claim this would be as ridiculous as saying that an explosion in a print factory could result in the complete and perfectly printed works of Shakespeare and the Bible! But if, as many of us know, God does exist, then is He really some uncaring deity who has wound up the world and just left it to run down somehow on its own? Or is He rather, as the Bible underlines so often, a God who cares about us so deeply that the very hairs of our head are numbered and our names are written on the palms of His hand?

So many times in the Bible God is spoken of as the God of the *individual* – the 'God of Abraham, of Isaac and of Jacob'. He says to each one of us 'I have *chosen* you', and yet how many of us hear that fantastic statement, let alone feel it in the very depth of our being? At best, if we know

Him, we may be able to convince ourselves that 'possibly' God loves us, but seldom that we are lovable by other people or worth anything in the world around us.

Channels only ...

I wish I could say that the church had heard this cry for help but in all honesty I am not convinced that it has. Significantly, one of the most effective posters outside a church in our area read simply MISSING YOU, WISH YOU WERE HERE ...

In fact, far from understanding the problem, we as Christians sometimes seem to make matters worse. So often we speak of ourselves as 'channels only' and 'instruments' for His will, thus seeming to miss out completely on the wonder of God's individual creation in our lives. Is it really possible for the God of all creation, who made every snowflake so beautifully and radically different from any other, to subscribe to this kind of thinking? When Christians speak of themselves as 'channels only' I have this terrible mental picture of a pile of grey drainpipes stacked unattractively and inanimately against a church wall!

But the characters in the Bible do not merge anonymously with a sort of holy mid-grey background. They stand out each and every one as a unique creation of the living God. .

Their stories were recorded because God worked through their *personalities* to do His will. He even worked through their faults to produce such *real* characters that they positively leap out from the pages of the Bible! Here were no amorphous grey channels, but men and women wholly and wonderfully freed to be themselves, with the life of God flowing through their veins.

Take Peter, the impulsive, over-confident fisherman, who was so sure he would never let his Master down, but who went out and wept like the rest of us when he panicked and denied his Lord.

Or David, the despised younger brother whom his father did not even bother to call when Samuel was looking for a new king of Israel. As Samuel passed by the stronger and more good-looking brothers, we see a very real and human picture of this small unimportant boy out watching his father's sheep on the hillside. No one else thought anything of David, but God was looking for someone to honour His name – someone who would become great by believing in Him.

Neither Peter nor David, nor Zacchaeus or Mary Magdalene ceased being *themselves* when they began to follow the Lord of life. On the contrary, for the first time ever, set free from their fears and failures, they became more truly themselves than they had ever been.

How do we measure our value?

Whereas in God's eyes our value lies in the fact that He made us and He loves us, and in the infinitely precious quality of human life, I think we as Christians often fall into the trap of accepting the world's yardstick for how much we matter as human beings.

Someone who is well known or important too often ranks an invisible 'ten points', whilst an out-of-work immigrant could score a pretty low mark. We do not mean to do this, but the values around us have unconsciously slipped into our thought patterns, just as they had in the time that James was writing the second chapter of his epistle.

Another yardstick often used is that of our outward appearance. Years ago now one of our children got quite upset at some film on television, when it became apparent that the hero was only devoted to the heroine because of how she looked. 'Does he only love her because she is beautiful?' was her indignant enquiry. Being quite a pretty little girl herself, she was only too well aware that the thoughts and feelings that went to make up her personality were not reflected in her appearance.

In reality, as we all know, the 'real me' inside has very little to do with what I look like, or how well known I am. A beautiful girl can be a pretty unattractive individual inside. Someone who is outwardly extremely articulate and well known for his ability may actually feel very unloved and unaccepted in *himself* and in his deeper needs and emotions.

Automatic labelling

Similarly we have tended to classify one another by the 'work' that we do. Ninety-nine times out of a hundred the question 'Who are you?' would receive an answer about the *job* we do in our daily lives – 'an engineer', 'a factory worker', 'an accountant', or 'just a housewife'.

Needless to say this does not tell other people a great deal about us except to give a general clue as to what to talk about, or in which direction our gifts or interest might lie. But many of us prefer things this way! To actually tell people about *ourselves*, our real interests or concerns, or worse still our deeper needs or feelings might be quite a frightening thought! Many of us would greatly prefer to stick to the 'automatic labelling system' – the work we do, the area we live in, the qualifications we have, the church we go to, and so on ...

But just consider for a moment what this kind of labelling does to the individual. Not only does it inevitably typecast that person as we categorise one another into little boxes, but there is an added and particular problem if the label itself is not a 'favourable' or 'acceptable' one.

Suppose that the answer to the question 'Who are you?' is 'an unmarried mother', 'a man who has been on the dole for several years', 'an immigrant in the back streets of Liverpool', 'a divorcee' or a 'punk on drugs'? What happens to the system then and is this all that we who are made in the image of God can see?

Whilst my husband was out of work for a whole year in the recent past, I was constantly aware of how difficult this was for other people to cope with. The pigeonhole was somehow missing, and they had no slot in which to put him! Even church people could often only talk about 'the job that he would shortly get in answer to prayer'. Now, as it happens, he did – but what of the many millions around the world who are not only out of work now, but will clearly remain so? What are we to answer to their question 'Do I really matter?'

What value does God give us?

One of the great distinguishing marks of the Christian faith has always been the immense value it attaches to human life. Hinduism, for instance, looks only towards the goal of Nirvana, where the individual will be merged into eternal oblivion – and human life is seen as just one more brief passing reincarnation, and very cheap.

But Jesus has told us that in His Father's house are many mansions, and He has gone to prepare a place especially for us. Moreover He was always at great pains to show His earthly followers how much He cared for them in this life, in the here and now.

'Not one sparrow ... can fall to the ground without your Father knowing it ... You are more valuable to him than many sparrows.'

Or again 'My sheep listen to my voice; I know them, and they follow me. I give them eternal life, and they shall never perish; no-one can snatch them out of my hand.'

Unfortunately popular science has once again got in the way of our thinking. People familiar with enormous world populations of many billions of people and mass computer technology cannot bring themselves to believe in a God who cares for the *individual* like this.

Even the present Archbishop of York has gone on record as saying that he cannot envisage God as some giant computer tuning in to every prayer and to the needs of the individual.

But if God created the universe, together with the human brain that invented the computer, is it not also highly likely that He is able to do, in the words of St Paul, 'more than we could ever ask or think'.

2

Selfishness or Self Discovery?

One of the diseases of this age is undoubtedly the search for self fulfilment and self gratification. We see it on our television screens each night as every viewer is encouraged to recognise his 'need' for a bigger and better car, a more glamorous holiday, or something to smoke or drink that will create the 'right' self image.

We see it in the divorce courts around the world, as one marriage after another breaks up because either party is not finding the self fulfilment that each is seeking at the other's expense. Or again in the endless battle between management and unions where both vie endlessly for a bigger and better slice of the cake - and neither is ever satisfied.

The neurotic search for fame, money or material comforts is often, I believe, a desperate effort to fill the hole in our lives that only God can fill. Or, in other words, it is often *because* people have never experienced deep down the wonder of God's love that this self-seeking mission continues.

Years ago whenever I was unhappy or depressed my first thought was always to go out and buy myself something new, however small. It was almost automatic and certainly, at the time, unconscious and, looked at logically, there was no way a new dress or some small item for the house could really make any lasting difference to my life! What I needed more than anything was to know that other people, and above all God Himself, really loved me and cared about me for myself. In my inability to see this I sought to take to myself material possessions, just as a child will beg for yet another new toy as a substitute for the love he really needs.

Self seeking such as this can reach really bizarre proportions, but it is never an answer. Just down the road from us lived one of the wealthiest men of this century. The entrance to Paul Getty's Tudor mansion was patrolled by armed guards to protect his immense wealth, but it is said that he died an unhappy man, never really knowing whether people wanted him for himself or his money.

I believe that such self seeking is really a cry for help in the absence of real love – but often the love has to come *first* before the self seeking can stop. In the story of Zacchaeus it was the love and acceptance of Jesus in going into the home of this despised and rejected man that released him to let go of the possessions which up till that moment had been the focal point of his life.

It is not only money that forms the centre of a search for self worth. 'Fame' is another familiar quest for recognition and identity today, but again it is a slippery slope for those who know it well.

I grew up on the edges of the international film industry. I was alongside people who were, and in some cases still are, household names, but there was nothing in their lives that could make me want what they had. Every step they took and every pronouncement they made was national news. Many of them never knew who their real friends were, and others lived in dread of what would happen when they became too old, or lost what talent they had. Most of these people had more than achieved the fame today's world hungers for, but as we saw all too clearly in the tragic deaths of people like Marilyn Monroe, Judy Garland and Elvis Presley, it never brought them true and lasting happiness.

So what do I mean by 'self discovery'?

Most Christians would prefer simply to say that this begins and ends at the foot of the cross, and that it is here alone we realise that we of ourselves are worth nothing, except that the Son of God loved us and gave His life for us. From that moment on it remains only for us to forget about ourselves, take up our cross and follow Him.

Doctrinally sound as this may be – and I do not myself question this – the resultant outworkings, *taken in a vacuum*, can be very cold comfort indeed.

Not long ago a friend of mine tried to bring to the attention of her vicar a woman in the congregation who was greatly in need of loving help and support, but he looked at her in blank amazement.

'But surely she is saved isn't she?' he said, as if that were the beginning and the end of the matter.

Happily such insensitivity is rare these days, but it hasn't yet disappeared altogether. And it is the kind of thing that makes people outside our churches think that we are only looking for heads to count in the congregation, and statistical conversions to the faith.

The secure person who has already experienced the loving acceptance of friends and family may well be able to roar ahead in his new-found faith. If he is genuinely and wholeheartedly 'seeking first the kingdom of God' then the love and the power from on high will quickly become a vibrant reality in his life.

It may never occur to him that *others* do not necessarily have the same experience. Hence it is only human to assume, rather judgementally, that such people are somehow 'lacking in their faith' or failing in their commitment.

But alas, for the many insecure and unwanted people who come to the church to find the love and forgiveness that they have never known, but that God has promised them, it may sometimes be a very different scene.

If someone has come to know the forgiveness of God, but still does not know that he is 'loved', or that he has any 'value' in himself, then clearly there is more that needs to be done. Coming to the foot of the cross is never an end but only a *beginning* to a whole new quality of life that the Lord has in store for us.

The paralysis of self consciousness

Moreover, the man who has never found himself is, paradoxically, constantly *'self* conscious'. Painfully unsure of himself, he is never really relaxed, still less full of joy of the Lord. One of the saddest things about not being free to be ourselves is the constant strain and tension under which we have to live as a result. If we are not able to relax in our own identity, being and saying what we really feel and believe, from the heart, then we will always be physically and mentally under stress. Instead of just enjoying the beauty of the scenery around us, or the pleasure of the company we are in, our whole being is taken up with a minute-by-minute struggle – 'What do they expect of me?', 'Will I come across as a good Christian?' 'What shall I say next?' and so on.

Someone like this is *already* selfish or self centred, because he is trapped within his own walls of fear. But never for one second does it occur to him that this prison is within *himself*, and that he has been called into the service of a God whose service is 'perfect freedom', but which he himself has never been let out to find.

If we then tell this person that he is to go out and give himself wholeheartedly to the service of Christ, we are asking the impossible. When the commandment tells him to 'love his neighbour as himself', the plain fact of the matter is that *he does not begin to love or accept himself*. In all probability he does not know who he really is or what gifts he has to give anyway.

How this affects our Christian life and witness

If we look at the life of the church today there are three primary ways in which we can see that self acceptance is not only important but crucial, both to our effective witness and to the whole quality of our spiritual lives.

If I do not feel loved or of any value, then I will inevitably feel that I have nothing to give to those around me. Far from the streams of living water springing up to eternal life, the barren emptiness within me will probably make me even resent the demands that I feel God and my fellow Christians are making of me.

It often seems to me that we are in too much of a hurry about Christian service. It is as if we have expected people to take one enormous leap over their own needs and hurts, and rush headlong into a life given up completely to others. Then a few years later we are surprised that many of them have given up, or are living joyless unfulfilled lives, simply going through the motions of their faith.

In St John's gospel we find the very clear instructions of Jesus given in the last few precious hours of His life. It seems safe to me to assume that these were of paramount importance, rather like a last will and testament to the young church that He was about to leave.

First of all (and remember that this was after *three solid years* spent in His company, listening to Him, and feeling loved and accepted by Him) they were to continue to 'live within my love' to 'love one another' as He had loved them.

Secondly He was not going to leave them 'comfortless'. They were to wait for change before they did *anything*. Before He finally ascended into heaven He told them 'Stay here in the city until the Holy Spirit comes and fills you ...' (Luke 24:49 The Living Bible) When they actually *experienced* the power and the love that Holy Spirit came to bring – not just 'learned about' or 'understood' but *experienced* – then they were sent out, but always in twos and threes, and with continuing instructions to love and care for one another.

In other words Jesus *never* expected his followers to go out feeling unloved or empty-handed.

Comparisons are odious

Another problem about attempting to serve God without knowing my own identity concerns the gifts and talents that have been given to me to use. If I feel unloved and of no intrinsic value, then the chances are that I will neither know nor appreciate the particular gifts that I have been given. Rather like the ugly duckling, I will always be comparing myself unfavourably with others, whilst not actually realising that my gifts are *different*.

Part of this is caused, as I said earlier, by accepting the worldly evaluation round us, and wishing that we were better looking, or that our gifts were more 'noticeable'. But a very large part is caused by people not affirming and encouraging one another's gifts within the body of the immediate group of friends.

Again, certain gifts are wrongly held up as more important, with an unspoken implication that everyone should be good at say preaching, or evangelism, whilst saying nothing about the priceless gifts of things like being able to make relationships easily, or organise the administration in the church.

The fall-out effect of not knowing our own gifts and being able to appreciate and work at them, is actually more devastating than we may realise. And it can be summed up in one rather ugly word – 'envy'.

I will never forget the horrible realisation, after several months of starting a successful outreach group with some friends in the area where we used to live, that there was someone in our midst who actually *resented* this.

Apparently she had tried to do it previously and failed. Instead of being able to rejoice in the new work God had

begun, her mind was full of quite bitter resentment
because she felt that *she* should have done this. It was not
long before we realised, and were able to tell her of the
many really lovely gifts that she *did* possess, but which
apparently no one else had either recognised or affirmed in
her. Today she is happily working away in quite a
different field, much more confident in her own identity,
and able to go out in love to those around her.

Going with the herd

The 'double-minded man', says James, is 'unstable in all
he does' – 'like a wave of the sea, blown and tossed by the
wind.'

This person, unsure of who he is, or what he really
thinks deep down, can easily be thrown up onto the shore
of almost anyone's opinion. And it is this aspect of
people's lack of identity and self worth that possibly
frightens me the most, especially where the church is
concerned.

This kind of Christian is a natural prey to 'Christianity'
as a sort of behaviour cult. Certain in himself that his *own*
needs or interests, even if he knows what they are, can
never be acceptable, he goes all out to conform with the
rest – adopting Christian 'in' language, staying in safe
Christian circles. He grinds his way on through life, not
full of joy but 'safe', and generally becomes more and more
bored with the whole scene, because for him it is a front
and not a reality. The trouble is that he could just as easily
be involved with the Moonies.

He does not know who he is.

There is no way that this person *can* live out a genuine
spiritual life without help, because he is primarily in
touch, not with God, but with what other stronger people
around him think. And because of this, even if he seems to

be trying, he cannot often hear the voice of God speaking to *him personally*.

His efforts to talk about his faith will only be reeled off parrot fashion, without the authentic stamp of a genuine 'heart' conviction, and certainly not in his own words because he really would not know what to say.

Perhaps all this sounds a rather heartless condemnation of the insecure person, and certainly he himself will probably be mostly unaware of the real situation. The trouble is, as I know from my counselling work, there are more people like this on the fringes of the church than we would like to think. And, after all, if *we* do not love and help them where else can they go?

It is not their fault, it is a natural result of life as they have experienced it - especially in the early years.

3

What Went Wrong?

As I sat listening to the problems of an eighteen-year-old
girl whose every movement announced the fact that she
felt unloved and unwanted, I was appalled by her negative
and twisted picture of God.

The more I pointed out His great love and concern for
her, the more she would counter this with seemingly every
verse in the Bible about His judgement and condemnation. It was really as if she *could* not see the other side of
the coin. And then I asked her what her earthly father was
like ...

From an early age he had pushed and bullied her to
work to achieve nothing but the very best. There had been
no fun, no relaxation, and above all no loving acceptance
of the child that God had given him. She was left with
nothing but a desperate awareness of his colossal
expectations of her, and above all his condemnation and
judgement of any failure to live up to these. Her picture of
God was almost identical.

Over and over again the Bible speaks of God as our
Heavenly Father, but sadly there are many people alive
who cannot bring themselves to use that word for the God
they have come to love – so bitter has been their earthly
experience of that role.

Parents are meant to be a 'visual aid' of God's love

Whether we like it or not, the fact of the matter is that as parents we will be providing a visual aid of God for our children. To the extent that they feel loved and accepted they will be able to grasp the concept of a God who lovingly wants the very best for them, but if they have been thoughtlessly hurt and damaged by lack of real love and acceptance the picture will be very different. So that before any real progress can be made in finding themselves lovingly accepted by their Heavenly Father, it may well be necessary for some deep process of inner healing to take place. The first thing is for us to be able to see God as He *really* is, and not as our own bitter and often sadly warped experiences may have led us to believe.

What is God really like?

Many years ago now, the Russians instructed one of their first Sputniks to keep a look-out for God when they were orbiting the earth. While most of us found this thought extremely funny, and wondered what they expected to see – perhaps an old Father-Christmas-like figure suspended somewhere out in the stratosphere – possibly we needed to and ought to be a bit more honest ourselves. For example, does our picture of God bear close examination in the light of the Bible version that is so clearly given to us?

Think of the loving father waiting longingly for the return of his prodigal son, watching faithfully day in, day out, and above all welcoming him home without judgement or condemnation. Or the caring shepherd searching all night, despite the many dangers around him, for the one sheep that was lost – despite the other ninety-nine safely tucked away in the fold. Can we honestly believe we do not *matter* to a God who cares for each one of us like this?

Is that your picture of God, or is there some way you are expecting Him to let you down, or to desert you in a crisis? Or do you perhaps feel that He is only interested in you when you are doing your Christian duty, and not in the small but vital everyday concerns that worry you in the small hours.

The attic

God comes into our lives through the attic area of our experience. Inevitably, since human nature is well and truly fallible, our parents will have made mistakes. They will have let us down when we most needed them, failed to understand us, and also in their enthusiasm to do 'the very best for us' they may well have made us feel unacceptable or not good enough into the bargain. To a greater or lesser degree this will be true for all of us, and clearly there is nothing very remarkable about this in itself. But consider the implications.

Have you ever noticed how many times in the New Testament Jesus speaks of His great love and closeness with His Father – the hours He willingly spends talking with Him up on the mountain tops? The tremendous assurance at all times of this union with the Father – 'I and my Father are one', 'I must be about my Father's business'. It is almost as if – indeed it *is* – that His life and power flowed out at all times directly from the Father in an unbroken stream. The rivers of living water flowed out to all those He met, and only for that one brief moment on the cross was He heard to say, 'My God, My God, why hast thou forsaken me?'

The blocks

Now the standard teaching has been that it is *sin alone* that stands as the block between us and the loving power that flows from our Heavenly Father. Once that sin is confessed and the barrier gone, the rivers of living water will flow out of our hearts, both for our own refreshment and for the benefit of those around us.

But is that our experience, and is sin the only block?

30

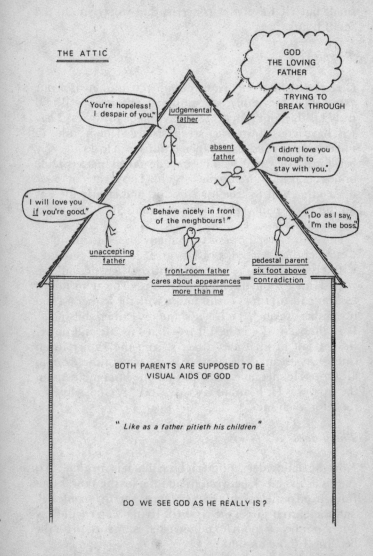

THE LIFE OF JESUS

FATHER

GOD THE HOLY SPIRIT

love   wisdom   power   peace

NO BLOCKS

Total parent
acceptance

" *This is my Beloved Son
in whom I am well pleased* "

"I and my Father are One"

JESUS

love's concern at all times
even on the way to the cross

peace at all times
however difficult

wisdom and understanding in
arguments with all comers

strength to overcome
even the satanic

" all power is given to me "
able to step out in faith
without fear

EVERYTHING FLOWS IN AN UNBROKEN STREAM
FROM THE FATHER

I believe that, to quote Selwyn Hughes in a recent series of 'Every Day with Jesus', many Christians lead lives of 'quiet desperation'. They have been told that the love and power of God is there for the asking, and that they have not because they ask not.

But when, as so often happens, they do *not experience* this heavenly lifeline as a reality, then they eventually begin to believe that somewhere along the line *they* have failed. If they risk asking for help they are usually told one of two things – either that they should 'have more faith', or that 'they should not expect to feel anything, because feelings are unreliable'.

Now of course at certain times in our lives our emotions are unreliable. But if God is love, then surely it makes no sense to say that we should not expect to feel this love *at all*!

In my own experience and the experience of numerous other people I have listened to, the blocks that prevent the life and love of God flowing into our lives and out to others correspond fairly exactly with the earthly blocks that existed in our own families.

A man whose father was distant and authoritarian, and too busy to spend time with his son on anything other than 'duty' matters, saw his Heavenly Father in the same light. He found it almost impossible – even quite frightening – to believe that God *loved* him (that was an embarrassing emotional and unmanly concept) and constantly laboured on to do his duty. He struggled on daily without the love and power that his Heavenly Father was longing to pour into his life.

A woman who was constantly told by her parents that she was not as good or as clever as her brothers and sisters found it impossible to believe that God accepted her *as she was*. Instead of being able to go out into the world in the freedom of His love, she was constantly comparing herself with other people to see where she had failed, and what others were thinking of her. Far from being able to love her

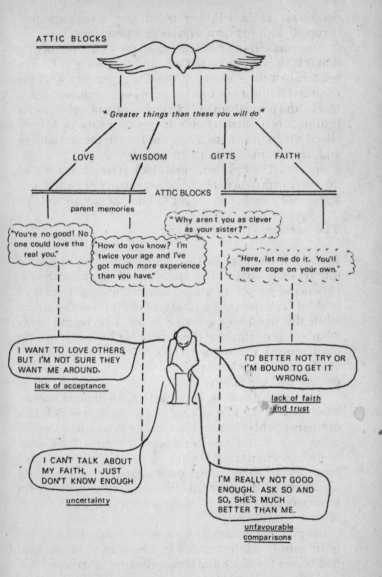

neighbour as herself, her mind was constantly preoccupied with her own worries and problems.

Now please don't misunderstand me – I am not saying
that it is impossible for the love and the power of God to
get through these blocks in our life experience – on the
contrary! It is just that until or unless we recognise them as
blocks and bring them to God, and to other Christians for
healing, then Satan is able to go on using them very
effectively to prevent us living our lives in the perfect love
and freedom that Jesus promises.

First of all we have to honestly look at whether or not we
do *really* experience the loving acceptance of God in our
lives – not whether we *ought to* but whether we *do*!

The transformation of real love

In the last few months I have seen a number of people
totally and wonderfully transformed by actually experiencing for the first time (often after many years of
faithful Christian service) that God really *loved* them. And
while this has been a great joy to see, I am bound to say
what a tragedy it is that this experience has taken so long
to enter into – and to wonder how many other people there
are in our churches who do not begin to know the
experience I am talking about.

A few years ago now, I came across a delightful woman
who radiated the love of God in everything she did. Her
ordinary earthly relationships with both men and women
were such that I was convinced she must have been
brought up in the most loving of homes. Over the years I
have learnt, like many counsellors, to guess fairly
accurately at the quality of love and acceptance meted out
to someone in childhood. Sadly, a great lack of such love is
often very evident.

Imagine my amazement, therefore, when she told me
quite calmly that her father had been an alcoholic who
had beaten her black and blue many times over – and that

she and her mother had seldom had a stable home or a safe refuge throughout her childhood. *But* the healing love of God had broken through all these bitter experiences, and in contrast she now lived her everyday life in the security of His caring and upholding presence at all times.

Surely the point is this – *I should not have been surprised!* The transformed life of this woman should not have been the exception but the rule. If we in the church believe in the healing and the freedom that the love of God has come to bring into our lives, then anyone, however bitter their past experiences, should be able to experience this healing and renewed sense of personal value.

We do not see Mary Magdalene creeping round after Jesus constantly thinking of herself as a failure or an outcast – on the contrary, she is radiant with the newly found love and acceptance of her Lord.

Nor is Zacchaeus perpetually full of remorse about the sinful extortionate life he has led. Once the love of Jesus has come into his house, he is set free to give and to part with the material 'props' he has clung to in compensation for the love he never knew.

What is different today?

Perhaps we have not understood or even wanted to understand what is going on deep down in the lives of some people.

Rather like the vicar I quoted earlier in the chapter, we have found it a great deal easier to put the problem fairly and squarely onto God's shoulders and leave it at that. In other words, once we have brought someone to the foot of the cross and to 'a new life in Christ', it has been much easier to feel that our own personal responsibilities have come to an end.

But what about the commands of Jesus to love one another as He has loved us, or to bear one another's burdens? The love of God in a broken life does not heal these bitter and earthly hurts overnight, without us playing our part. So far as we can see Mary Magdalene was allowed to remain close to her Lord throughout the rest of His earthly life – and to be the first to see Him after He rose from the grave.

We have to really love and support one another in the name of Christ, as we have been commanded to do, if some of these blocks are to be wholly and permanently removed from our lives. Hurts that have taken a lifetime to make us into what we are will never be healed in a day or even a year, and a great deal more loving support and inner healing may be needed.

What we have done is to 'spiritualise' the problem and leave it at that. If someone has come into a saving knowledge of God then we imply that he should *already have become* a new creature – not just 'spiritually' with the beginning of a new quality of eternal life but *actually, humanly*, in the *here and now*. Full stop. Our responsibility is over and the problem can now be left to God to deal with. Sigh of relief. We are often taught that when we come to the foot of the cross we shall *automatically experience* the wonder of God's love for us. *Actually*, sometimes we do and sometimes we don't. The same is true of the coming of the Holy Spirit upon us for service. There is no problem with this, as clearly it didn't always happen in the early church either (Acts 19:2). The problem lies in our not being free to *say what we really experience, what we still need, and where we still hurt.*

Perhaps if we are being really honest we should add that quite a lot of people in our churches might not want to hear the true situation stated openly either, simply because they wouldn't be sure what to do next.

Hence the fact that many of us have got stuck in the trap of what I will call 'plastic' or 'front-room' Christianity, which really amounts to doing our best to keep up appearances in our own strength.

4

Front-Room Christianity

Not long ago I read a very convincing article, pleading that we were all far too preoccupied with the subject of 'wholeness' and that we should be aiming first and foremost at true holiness. But if we do not actually *experience* the love and power that Jesus came to bring – not because of lack of faith, but because of deep hurts in our past that affect our relationship with God – then surely we must be made whole before we can even begin to 'be' holy.

Holiness is not some kind of additive, suspended like a Pre-Raphaelite halo, untarnishable above our heads! It has to begin in the very depths of our being, or it will not begin at all.

'Virtue is only easy,' says Richard Foster, 'to the extent that God's gracious work has taken over our *inner* spirit, and transformed the ingrained habit patterns of our lives. Until that is accomplished, virtue is hard, very hard indeed. We struggle to exhibit a loving and compassionate spirit, yet it is as if we are bringing something in from the outside. Then bubbling up from the inner depths is the one thing we did not want, a biting and bitter spirit.'[1]

There is a lovely story about a famous Scots preacher who was approached by a very enthusiastic woman after

[1] Richard Foster, *Celebration of Discipline*, Hodder and Stoughton, p. 7.

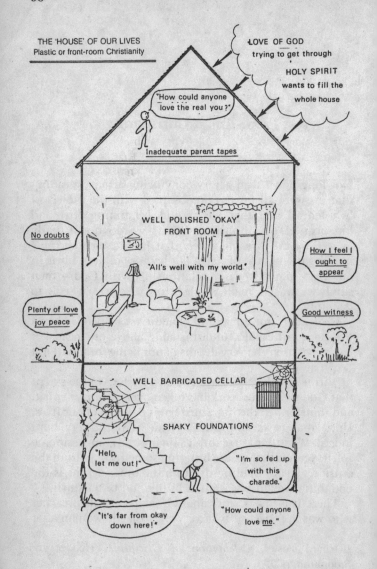

he had delivered a particularly moving and helpful sermon.

'Oh pastor,' she exclaimed, 'what a wonderful sermon, and what a truly lovely man you are.'

'Madam,' he replied, with typical Scots candour, 'if you could see in my heart you would spit in my face.'

(How true for many of us, but how few would ever dare to admit to this!) Most of us have been brought up to behave 'nicely', not to let the neighbours see our nasty habits. We learn quite early in life that there must of necessity be a gap between what we are really like and how we appear to other people, although this will probably be quite unconscious and just a well-ingrained habit pattern.

The cover of respectability

The reasons for feeling we must display this outer shell of respectability are perfectly understandable.

Watching a whole load of scruffy-looking children pouring out of school all screaming and yelling at one another is, naturally, not thought by the headmaster to be a good advertisement for the educational establishment in question!

And a spoilt child creating a scene in the supermarket, because her mother has not bought her another packet of her favourite sweets, does nothing for the family in question – although most of us have had to go through this embarrassing situation at one time or another!

Unfortunately it is only human for us to be more concerned about how our children behave *in public*, or when they are on show, than about how they *are* and how they feel deep down.

In addition to this, we have all been affected by the rather plastic 'image-making' of the age. The packaging of every product on the market has a very high priority in the consumer world, and this is even true for pop stars and politicians.

A beautifully presented can of luscious-looking fruit, on which the manufacturers have lavished hours of careful cosmetic attention, will, as everyone knows, sell much better than one with a plain label saying simply 'tinned peaches'.

But, however good the label, the vital question must still be about the quality of the contents. If the can is rusting away on the inside, so that the peaches are anything but appetising to the taste, then the label is a waste of time.

Whatever the reason, some of us become quite adept at this kind of cover-up activity, and the 'front rooms' of our lives are nicely decorated with spotless wallpaper and well-polished smiling furniture – and no one is ever allowed to see what is in the cellar area. After all, we will probably have been told often enough as children that no one would like us if they knew what we were *really* like!

The habit goes on

The trouble is that when we become Christians it is all too easy to carry this sort of behaviour pattern on without even noticing. We are told, for example, that a Christian should be full of the joy and peace of the Lord. But if we do not actually know this peace, we may well feel that of course we must pretend that we do. Just as it was at school or at home, we feel obliged to put on an appearance of good Christianity for the sake of our witness to others – to do anything else would be letting the side down.

Furthermore, if my experience is anything to go by, the chances of our doubts or problems being lovingly accepted, if we do ever risk talking about them, are definitely on the low side. My first experience of trying to share my needs in this way was enough to put me off for life!

Soon after we got engaged my husband was sent off to India for six months, and literally within hours of his arrival on the last plane up to Assam, the Chinese invaded. I was a very young Christian at the time, and had already experienced a number of painful bereavements in my life. Both my parents and my only brother were dead by the time I was seven, and a much-loved boyfriend had committed suicide after being sent down from university. Needless to say, this new situation with Peter firmly in the firing line brought me close to breaking point – and I made the fatal mistake of actually admitting this to another Christian.

'Oh,' she said, with what I can only describe as righteous indignation, 'surely you ought to be able to trust God with something like that.' So that, when all I needed was a bit of loving caring support in my flagging faith, I was left feeling totally unacceptable, and also dreadfully guilty for ever daring to admit to such fears as a Christian.

I wish I could say that such instances are untypical, but alas I could repeat similar stories with many different variations from my few short years of counselling.

Starting from a position of reality

If we can't share our *real* selves and our *real* feelings with other people, then how can we ever know that we are *really* loved?

In a way it is rather like the Indian Five Year Plan, which would start on the next five years from where the country 'ought to have got to' rather than where it actually was! In Hinduism 'reality' exists up above, and real life is only a poor earthly 'imitation'. Therefore you always start from the 'ideal' situation rather than the actuality.

But it is not possible to grow in our Christian lives or in our relationships unless we start from a basis of rock-solid truth. If we have doubts and fears, then clearly these will not go away unless someone helps us. Moreover, a good veneer of front-room Christianity is more easily recognisable for what it is than we think.

The commands of Jesus were that we should be 'salt' and 'light' in the community around us. In other words that our *whole lives* were to show forth the love and the healing power of God. To me this implies that we should be letting God take over the whole quality and depth of our life structure, so that the resulting difference is clearly visible to everyone. Taking the analogy of the house again, His light must be allowed to shine into *every* corner, *including* the dark and cobwebby areas we do not wish to show to anyone. Those painful and sinful cellar corners, where all the doubts and fears, hurts and anger are hidden away – and where they will remain unless they are brought to the light for His healing.

When we have done this, to quote Richard Foster again, 'Divine Love has entered our inner spirit and taken over our habit patterns. In the unguarded moment there is a spontaneous flow from the inner sanctuary of our lives of "love, joy, peace, patience, kindness, goodness, faith-fulness, gentleness and self-control." (Gal. 5:22,23) No longer is there the tiring need to hide our inner selves from others. We do not have to work at being good and kind, we *are* good and kind.'

Free to 'be' salt and light

One of the most effective sales gimmicks of the eighties seems to be the 'free trial' examination syndrome, on the fairly safe basis that once we have handled the article for ourselves we shall then find it extra hard to resist. And if we are really at large in the world as 'lights' so that others can see our God qualities – even although we will inevitably make mistakes and show up our failings – then there should be no doubt as to our effectiveness.

But one of the things that disturbs me greatly is the number of Christians who seem afraid to mix with those around them in their normal surroundings. Preoccupied with a picture of themselves as 'strangers and pilgrims', they exist in the world but are often so tucked away in their 'ghettos' that they remain well and truly insulated against the cold draughts of everyday life around them.

Is it because they are afraid of contamination? Is it the danger that their lives might not stand the test of their words? Or is it simply that they do not, with their inner uncertainty, know how to be 'themselves' anyway, and are not sure what is expected of them?

Alas, many Christians are often made to feel that living freely in a relaxed sort of way in the world around them is not 'right'.

The most telling story I have ever heard illustrating this point came from Murray Watts at a recent Greenbelt seminar:

Many years ago a man left his own village in the mountains to visit a town far away. When he got there after weeks of hard and dusty travelling, he quickly discovered that they had the most amazing secret of Life. Before long he came to understand the secret for himself and to make it his own. His excitement knew no bounds, and he could not wait to rush back and tell the people in his own village – but they would not let him go.

'Wait here,' they said, 'until you have learnt the right words in which the secret must be told to others.' And so he waited for many long weeks, until the words were his, when again he was keen to be off and tell his friends about the secret of Life he had found.

'Ah no,' they said, 'for you have many more things to learn ... People who travel with the secret must dress as we do and put on different clothes to speak about it.' And so he waited yet again until he looked exactly as they looked, and could have been mistaken for one of them, and once again he urged them to let him go, for the secret was very important.

'Just one more thing,' they said, 'and then you can be off. There is a certain kind of behaviour that befits the people of the secret, which you really must learn before you leave us.' And so our friend sat down again to study their behaviour, their customs, their mannerisms, and then finally they said to him, 'Now you are ready to go.'

As he hurried over the mountains and down the valleys, his excitement knew no bounds because of what 'the secret' would mean to the people of his village. Finally after many weeks his own dear village came into view perched high upon the mountain he had come to know so well. He ran joyfully towards it, calling out as he went ...

The villagers looked down from their mountain walls in amazement. Who on earth was this strange-looking creature running towards them shouting so loudly and in such peculiar words? They became very worried and called out the village elders, who urged him to go away. He shouted all the more, but not a single soul recognised him or understood what it was he was saying. Finally, since he would not go of his own accord, they took up stones to throw at him, telling him to go away and never come back.

Battered and bleeding he set off on the long journey back to the town of the secret, weeping as he went about the rejection he had experienced, and the lost opportunity to talk about the secret. When at last he reached the town he poured out the bitter experiences he had been through, but to his amazement they were not surprised.

'You have been persecuted for the "secret",' they told him. 'And this is a part of the cost we have to pay. Never mind, dry your tears, and come and settle down here with us where it is safe, in the town where the secret belongs.'

The dangers of unreal witness

The story is so powerful that there is really nothing to add. But in my own experience *more than half* of the people I have talked to outside of our churches have been put off coming to the possibility of a real faith, *not* by the truths of the gospel, but by the unreal witness and churchianity displayed by people who call themselves Christians.

We must start where John starts in his first epistle with a totally genuine and real personal witness, whether this contains problems or not –

'I myself have seen him with my own eyes and listened to him speak. I have touched him with my own hands. He is God's message of Life.'

And I believe the world is, not unreasonably, making the same demands of us. People just want to come alongside us as friends, to find out what we really believe, and what kind of light we shed. They do not mind if we express the occasional doubt or uncertainty for this is part of the stamp of reality. In fact there are a great many parts of our 'not-so-fantastic Christian experience' that I personally believe we both can and should share with others in order to help them find the truth. Real-life experiences that should be a natural part of our 'front-room' furniture, along with the beautiful and well-polished variety.

I will never forget the first time this lesson was brought home to me. We were having a meeting in our house to which many friends and neighbours had been invited. An Australian evangelist had been speaking about his faith in clear down-to-earth English and many people had been helped. But as the meeting broke up, one young preacher stayed on, arguing with and challenging some of the Christians present about seemingly every problem in the book concerning the possibility of faith. It was all rather like a game of verbal ping-pong, and it seemed to me that they were getting nowhere fast. Every word he said was convincing me that his *real* problem with faith had very little to do with all the textbook arguments he was putting up.

At the time I was halfway though a Christian counselling course and had recently had to face up to a

number of doubts and fears that I had never owned to
before. In fact I had only just got back onto solid ground in
the discovery that God had been with me all the time – it
was simply my picture of Him that had been wrong.

Eventually as the fairly pointless verbal battle looked
like going on into the small hours, I plucked up the
courage to speak. Typically the problem I had with this
was not so much what *he* would think, but that none of my
Christian friends present had any idea of what I had been
going through and might well be shocked!

When I finally told him that I had only recently
experienced many similar doubts and problems, and
strugglingly made my way back to a much stronger faith
from a position of absolute honesty, he rounded on me
with totally justifiable anger.

'Well, why on earth didn't you say so before?' he
demanded. 'And we could have saved ourselves all this
pointless argument!'

It was a lesson I would not forget.

The truth of the matter is that often our rather synthetic
problem-free faith actually keeps some people away from
finding the truth. The feeling is, not unnaturally, that
they could never be that 'good' or that 'certain'. Once we
start to admit that we also sometimes have problems and
needs, then they can begin to identify with us and come
alongside.

For over two years I took part in a late-night TV
Christian chat show, which went out every day. The wide
variety of people involved were from different age groups,
different backgrounds and different denominations, but
they were all chosen because they were prepared to be
themselves, warts and all, on the air – not an easy thing,
especially if you happen to live in the local area of
viewing.

During the many hundreds of programmes we did
people shared all kinds of things, never attempting to hide
the difficulties and fears they experienced, as well as the

joy and strength of their faith. I do not believe that it was any accident that the viewing figures remained consistently high, particularly amongst those who never darkened the door of any church. Many letters spoke of compulsive viewing and a recognition that here at last was something they could identify with, that was not smothered in holy language and unreal witness.

Predictably not a few Christians voiced their anxiety about the programme, because it did not carry a clear 'message' every night.

Whilst we are papering over the cracks in our Christian 'front rooms' to make it appear that all is well with our faith … that life is pure joy, with a simple and direct answer to every prayer, there is no doubt in my mind that outsiders would accept our witness far more readily if we could get down on their level and admit that sometimes *we* do not understand either, or that there are days when God seems far away from *us* as well.

God does not need our protection

It is almost as if we feel we need to protect God or defend His name, or that possibly He might even disappear in a puff of smoke if we look too closely – like the terrible day when it actually dawned on us that there was no Father Christmas! But surely Almighty God is far greater than the sum of all our fears and doubts …

He will take what we are and what we offer Him – our failings and our gifts, our needs and our strengths, and transform them for us in His service – *if only we will let Him*.

We are not called to be plaster saints, but real flesh-and-blood witnesses. For surely this is one of the great attractions of the Bible – that it does not attempt to paper over the cracks in the lives of its principal characters. They are good and human, with a liberal sprinkling of the failures that beset us all.

There is no attempt at a cover-up of the lamentable denial by Peter at the High Priest's house, or of the terrible story of the great King David, who had a man murdered because he fancied his wife. These people are *there* in scripture to enable us to acknowledge our *own* weaknesses, and to come closer to the only *One* who can really help us change these by His strength.

In these and so many other ways we belie the fact that *our* God is too small! There is no way that we can possibly 'protect' Him, but the only way that we can really serve Him is to allow Him to come into the depths of our being and clear out the cellar area. Then and only then will we become the 'salt' and the 'light' that He has commanded us to be.

While we are busy keeping our problems and our failings well hidden away in the cellars of our lives, that telling sentence, 'I can't hear what you say, because what you *are* speaks so loudly,' sums up the problem exactly.

5

Clearing out the Cellar

Not many houses these days are lucky enough to have cellars, but for those that do these are grade one dumping areas. Where else to hide all that jumble waiting for the next sale; Aunt Agatha's dreadful lamp (until her next visit!) or the terrible mess left over from that carpentry effort of the children's that went so badly wrong? The problem is that what we stack down in the cellar never just goes away of its own accord – it is always there waiting for our next visit, or threatening to overflow the house if one more thing gets pushed down there! Moreover, it may be out of sight, but it is seldom out of mind!

If cellars made of bricks and mortar are bad when overfull, then emotional flesh-and-blood cellars are considerably worse.

Down here in these cobwebby precincts you will find all the bad and unacceptable feelings stacked away ... For some reason the British in particular have grown up with the idea that you must never give way to fear, anger or tears. While the Arabs and the Italians bewail and lament their sorrows, and rant and rave at all comers, the British have seldom felt it right even to be seen to cry at the funeral of a loved one.

A friend of mine who runs her company welfare department told me recently how, if she had to tell an Italian employee bad news of any kind, it was essential to first shut all the doors and get out the box of tissues, and

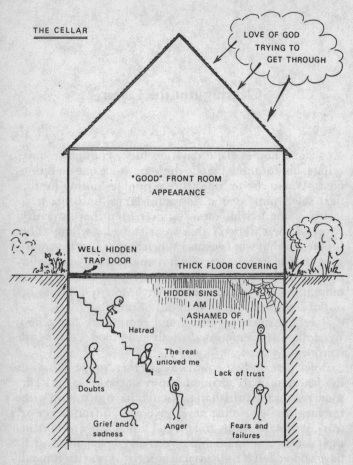

What lurks in the cellars of our lives affects the whole house

God wants to shine the light of His love
into every corner

even then the whole factory knew what was going on!

Perhaps we despise this kind of overt behaviour, but at least we have to see that they get their feelings out of their system. Pushing those same feelings down out of sight will not make them go away, but instead they will probably remain with us for many years to come, playing havoc with our minds and bodies. Then there are all those very specific memories and fears that we have never risked telling anyone about, but which tend to creep up on us in the small hours. The anger about how we were treated as children, the hurt of feeling rejected in favour of a brother or sister, or the sense of never really being loved for what we were ...

For most of us these are just ugly and unhappy memories that would be much better brought to the light for His healing touch – and for the love and acceptance of others. But for some the hurts are deeper and more traumatic than that and not to bring them up to the light of day constitutes a real danger that we ignore at our peril.

Helen was an active member of a well-known fellow-ship group in London, who gradually began to drift into a greater and deeper depression as the days went by. Strugglingly she tried to tell her friends in the group what she was going through and how bad it was getting. They were predictably shocked. 'We are praying for you,' said one of them. 'You must have more faith,' said another. And what she in fact had was a very severe breakdown.

Today she has completely recovered, but not through any miracle cure. It has taken several years of loving support from two families, and a caring group that was prepared to listen to how bad it felt – and not to shove those feelings quickly back into her cellar area, mainly I'm afraid for their own peace of mind.

If the feelings and fears that lurk below our cellar floorboards are sufficiently traumatic, and if we are not able to go down and face them honestly in good company, then we will inevitably pay the price in the end. And if this is in a breakdown situation, then we are effectively catapulted down through the floorboards to face everything at once – and needless to say, when we are in no condition to do so.

In my own case, as with a great many others, the hidden emotions never quite got to breakdown level, but looking back I can see how they affected and overshadowed my whole life, preventing me from ever knowing the meaning of real joy, or the love and acceptance of other people.

For years I had no idea of what it was like to live in the present. I was always looking forward to the next holiday, hoping the next year would be better – that somehow, somewhere, I would discover what real happiness meant. Moreover this situation continued for many years after I became a Christian, and even after I experienced the power and love of the Holy Spirit – although looking back now I believe that this was the beginning of the healing process.

Shutting out pain shuts out life

The series of bereavements that I had experienced as a child was so devastating that I don't ever remember crying about it – there was just nothing but a hopeless trackless wasteland ahead of me. So that many years later the cellars of my life were still full to bursting with pain and grief that had never been allowed to see the light of day. Each succeeding year was a dull heavy experience seen through the dark glass of painful memories that took away all the colour and the joy.

There was absolutely no room for the healing love and the joy that God longed to pour in, until the cellar area was cleared out – but of course I had no idea of this at the time! Eventually the pressure became so great that the cellar doors were no longer able to contain the pain.

It all started with the death of my neighbour's husband in a plane crash. As I went down the road to try and comfort her, and listen to her very real grief, I discovered to my horror that my feet were like lead. This 'good Christian neighbour' simply did not want to face her pain, and without realising the reason, I was simply horrified by my reaction.

Shortly afterwards, and following a series of other bereavements around my family and friends, the flood gates began to open. Suddenly I found myself in almost uncontrollable floods of tears over every sad book or film, and often for no particular reason as well.

My husband, who like all good Englishmen had been brought up to believe that emotions were not something you ever talked about, let alone expressed in this rather obvious and embarrassing way, was suitably horrified! 'What on earth is the matter?' he would protest as I flooded my way through yet another box of tissues in an impossible jellified heap of grief!

But gradually, as I cried and cried, I discovered a very strange thing. Somewhere along the line the sky had actually become a brighter blue and the spring green leaves of the trees were the most beautiful thing I had ever seen. For the *very first time* those everyday things that had been there all my life were actually becoming a part of *my experience*, instead of just being seen through a glass darkly. Before I used only to paint and write about them, but now they actually entered into my life in full glorious technicolour. For years this great weight of grief had stood between me and any possibility of experiencing the good and beautiful things around me – and the contrast was something I will truly never forget!

When the Holy Spirit of God enters a life He wants to inhabit the whole area. He knows that until we give our whole selves to Him, without any attempt at pretence or cover-up, then we shall never be free to become the people He wants us to be – and we shall never know the 'abundant life' that Jesus promised us.

I am convinced that this is one major reason why so many people do not grow in their Christian lives – because they start from a position of where they feel they 'ought to be', rather than where they really *are*. Inevitably the strain of building onto the fabric of 'pretence' rather than just allowing God to extend His life into the cellar area of reality makes this kind of building pretty hard going and unattractive.

Why isn't it mentioned in the Bible?

People often ask me why, if this is so important, there is not more written about it in the Scriptures. The Old Testament speaks of God desiring 'truth in the inward parts', and John reminds us that we are to 'love one another in deed and in truth'. However, I am convinced that the primary reason is that for anyone living in the Middle East this kind of instruction was simply not necessary. As I said earlier, many other nations give vent to their emotions with complete freedom. Jesus Himself wept over Jerusalem, and at the tomb of His friend Lazarus, and was not remotely embarrassed to express His righteous anger when driving out the money-changers from the temple. To tell a Jew or an Arab that he should let his feelings out without pretence would be like telling him that he should breathe!

In our society, anger and temper tantrums, for example, have to be put down into the cellar area pretty early in life because people around us can't cope with the fallout effect. But it is one thing to handle our anger and frustration in such a way that it does not harm other people – it is quite another to smother these feelings altogether and deny them at all costs. After all, anger is usually about something that needs dealing with, and frustration indicates a need to redirect our energies away from unhelpful restrictions.

As with tears and grief, many people find it difficult to cope with the overt expression of anger – I do myself. But it is one thing to say, 'Look, I'm sorry, but I just can't cope with that – please go and be angry somewhere else, or beat your pillow with it.' It is quite another to say, 'All anger is wrong – "nice" people never feel angry.'

If we never allow ourselves to experience the feeling of anger then the chances are that we shall be unable to stand up for ourselves or for the faith we believe in. Jesus did not quietly creep into His Father's temple when it was being abused by the money-changers, and ask them with a sweet gentle smile if they would mind terribly moving out. In fact the rather sickly Sunday School image of 'Gentle Jesus meek and mild' has left us with what to my mind is an erroneous and unmanly picture of the Son of God when He walked this earth.

As I read it, the Bible instructions are 'Be ye angry, and sin not' (Eph.4:26) – which to me means that we should face it, get rid of it, but make sure that it does not harm anyone else.

Learning to handle negative cellar emotions

When I said to a very unhappy and depressed woman that I would not be content until I saw her get in touch with her hidden anger about all that had happened to her, she looked horrified. How could a good Christian say such a thing?

On the outside she was a mild compliant sort of person, allowing people to walk all over her and make quite unreasonable demands on her time, but occasionally I would catch that flash of anger about how she was really feeling deep down. What she did for others was not given out of the love and joy of a full heart, but in resignation and despair, because she felt that she had no right to ever say no to anyone.

Depression is often caused by hidden and unexpressed anger because the effort of keeping these negative emotions barricaded in the cellar takes up a great deal of energy. Also, as with buried grief or anxiety, the good and spontaneous reactions to life have to get barricaded down there as well – all our emotions must be well concealed if we go in for this sort of cover-up.

This particular woman had suffered all her childhood from a very angry and demanding father who had never allowed her to speak up for herself or have any opinions of her own. Not surprisingly she despised the very hurtful anger she had had to live with, as well as continuing to feel that she had 'no right' to any needs or feelings of her own. She had learnt to be a doormat very early in life, and had simply carried this behaviour pattern on into her Christian life because she had thought that this was what was meant by 'turning the other cheek'. It never occurred to her that God was *not* angry and demanding like her father, but that actually He really loved and cared about her every need, longing that she would find the freedom and spontaneity of His abundant life.

Moreover, she was attempting to hide her angry feelings from a God who inevitably knew all about them anyway! When I pointed out that Jesus had already taken the sin, the rejection and the anger of the whole world on Himself when He hung on the cross, and that He was more than able to take hers as well, I could see the light begin to dawn.

When she did finally get in touch with all this hidden anger it came in the most enormous burst, and so far as I can recollect it was over something quite trivial! But certainly one or two people close to her had a pretty uncomfortable time for a while – and my guess is that they deserved it!

Suddenly she was able to stand up for herself, to say what she really felt, and to resist the intolerable pressures that people had unknowingly put upon her. Today she is a lively, enthusiastic, outgoing sort of person who radiates a genuine giving joy in all that she does.

In a very helpful book entitled *The Betrayal of the Body* by Alexander Lowen (published by Collier) this kind of person is shown diagrammatically in a sort of amoeba-shaped form, which can be interpreted as follows:

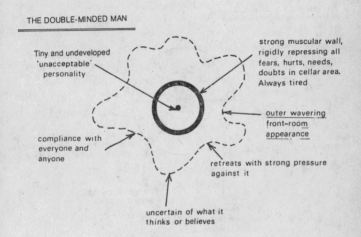

THE DOUBLE-MINDED MAN

Tiny and undeveloped 'unacceptable' personality

strong muscular wall, rigidly repressing all fears, hurts, needs, doubts in cellar area. Always tired

outer wavering front–room appearance

compliance with everyone and anyone

retreats with strong pressure against it

uncertain of what it thinks or believes

The real genuine (cellar) self is firstly very tiny and almost unrecognisable, but more important it is rigidly contained in the cellar by a thick impenetrable muscular layer that spends all its effort and energy on concealment and nothing more. Such an individual is constantly tired or under pressure, with no energy or enthusiasm left for living. The outer line of identity is unsure, constantly shifting, and moves with each new pressure against it. For example, before I expressed the grief bottled up in my own cellar area, I was constantly tired and depressed with no enthusiasm for life. But once the feelings had been let out, with no need to hold them in any more, I was set free to be myself – together with all the energy for living that had previously been used for containment.

The healthy individual, on the other hand, looks like this –

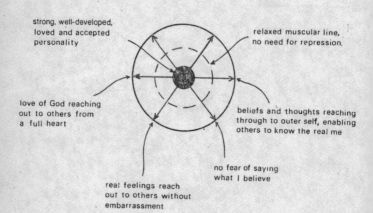

THE HEALTHY INDIVIDUAL

strong, well-developed, loved and accepted personality

relaxed muscular line, no need for repression.

love of God reaching out to others from a full heart

beliefs and thoughts reaching through to outer self, enabling others to know the real me

no fear of saying what I believe

real feelings reach out to others without embarrassment

His inner self is reasonably developed, the muscular line is there but only light since it has no need rigidly to control what is inside, and all his genuine thoughts, feelings, and responses are able to reach right through to the outer person that others can see and relate to. In other words, both he and his friends are aware of who he *really* is, and what he believes and thinks – without fear of rejection or disagreement. This is no double-minded man, but a well-adjusted, secure individual who is able to go out and relate to others around him with love and acceptance.

Certainly he will be far from perfect, like the rest of humankind, but as his *real* needs and feelings come to the surface they can be dealt with by God and others in His name – above all there will be no cover-up, no misspent energy keeping the cellar area barricaded!

Facing our fears

Other well-known cellar inhabitants are the fears and fantasies of childhood.

Just as the buildings and places we remember from early childhood as 'enormous' and 'impressive' often turn out, when revisited in later life, to be quite small and insignificant-looking, so it is with fears that were buried at an early age.

Fear of the dark, fear of some terrible impending 'thing' that may come to pass, fear of punishment if we are found out – all these can mount up in our subconscious till they become like some vast mountain paralysing us and preventing us from stepping out freely into God's new day.

Such fears are particularly bad for those whose families live in their grip as well. I remember one girl whose mother had communicated to the whole family quite early in life that she lived in dread of something really terrible happening to them. If at all possible she would never travel in the same car, every thing was triple-locked at night to keep out the intruders she was certain were going to come, and of course she was always warning the children to be *very very* careful wherever they went ... Not surprisingly Sarah had grown up as a jittering heap of nerves who found herself quite unable to even begin to experience the 'peace of God that passes all understanding'.

But as we talked about each experience, and every fear that haunted her nights and her dreams, facing each one for what it really was in the clear light of day, they gradually began to come down to size. We were then able to ask God to remove them one by one. It took a while, but as time went by her face began to clear, her frightened nervous air relaxed, and she really began to experience the peace that God was longing to give her.

None of these things would have been possible without

facing the negative feelings in question. So long as they are allowed to inhabit the cellar areas of our lives, no amount of prayers for 'love, joy and peace' will simply remove them. But when we go down the dark and slippery steps with someone to love and help us in God's name, then for the first time we will be able to face up to and get rid of all these, and many other, 'unacceptable' emotions we have stored away down there.

Hiding away our sins

Of course fears and feelings are not the only inhabitants of these murky cellar precincts. Many of the things we put down here we would much rather not show to *anyone* - although we will probably reluctantly acknowledge that the all-seeing eye of God must know about them.

The snag about this is that very often we need help in dealing with our sins as well. The Holy Spirit can usually be relied upon to point them out to us - that is to say, if we haven't managed to harden our consciences against even these promptings. But actually, since we have been told to confess our sins to one another, we do often need to be reassured that God has forgiven some of these dark and murky corners of our lives.

We also need to be encouraged to see that we are not alone, and that others have some pretty nasty failings as well. Again this is another very important reason for not maintaining the 'plaster-saint' front-room Christianity that I spoke about earlier.

Notice for example how often Paul speaks of his faults and failings when he of all people might have had reason not to! If you think about it he had probably been responsible for putting to death friends and relations of many of the people he was speaking to - but he does not attempt to cover this up.

I am more and more aware that often the only way to release people to speak about *any* of the cellar areas in their lives is to share my *own* experiences. What right do I have to cover up what God has done for me?

When I have shared things that have happened to me, faults that I find it difficult to conquer, or fears that I have experienced, this seems to act like a catalyst for others around me. It is almost like throwing a stone in a pond, when you can actually watch the ripples spreading out further and further as people are set free to look into their *own* cellars in the realisation that *they are not alone*.

6

How Do We Find Our Real Identity?

For many years our rabbit and guinea pig have lived together in the same run. And since the guinea pig moved in there when he was extremely small, he clearly suffers from some kind of identity problem which makes him think he ought to hop like a rabbit! It may seem a silly illustration, but I really wonder how many of us are trying to hop when we were never meant to!

How many of us have not at some time secretly wished that we were like that Christian who is such a good speaker, that girl down the road whom everyone seems to like, or that other friend who is so good-looking? And even if we do eventually accept our own gifts, is it not rather in the nature of 'well, let's grin and bear it, because we've got no alternative'? So that, far from accepting ourselves, we are judging God for not giving us a better deal, and writing off our own talents, or lack of them, because they aren't up to our requirements.

I love the story of the woman who came in great distress to her minister one morning. She was deeply convinced, she said, that God wanted her to become an evangelist – but alas it was impossible for her to fulfil this calling, because she had so many children to look after. The minister was undaunted. 'How wonderful,' he said, 'that God has not only called you to this work, but has also given you a ready-made congregation.'

Self-confidence or self-acceptance?

For years it was thought quite wrong to encourage
children to think positively about their achievements.
Criticism of failure was far more important than
encouraging them because they had done well. After all,
this was hardly likely to produce humility, and it would be
simply terrible to have a child around that was over-
confident.

As Christians I believe we are still guilty of the same
thought patterns. We have confused self confidence – that
is to say thinking too highly of ourselves because we have
taken personal credit for the abilities and attributes we
have been given – with self acceptance, or recognising and
owning the talents we do have and feeling 'okay' and
accepted for who we are as a result.

If you look at the letters of Paul, he does not mince
words about his gifts or his attributes – or even what he has
been through for the Lord's sake. Neither does he pat
himself on the back! He simply accepts that these are the
talents and experiences he has 'on board' as a part of his
personality, but that the knowledge and love of God is far
more important.

In our enthusiasm not to think too highly of ourselves
we have tended to overlook *both* the *value of the
individual as a human being, and the importance of the
gifts he has been given*.

The result has not been genuine loving humility, but
paralysing self rejection and envy of others! Hundreds of
thousands of talents going to waste for lack of recognition
and affirmation.

The mirror image

It has been said that we can only truly see ourselves as a
mirror reflection in the eyes of someone else. Inevitably
this begins in the family home where we experience what

our parents, and our brothers and sisters really think of us! And in an alarmingly high proportion of cases this experience does more harm than good! The best families are those in which each child is helped from a very early age to see his *own particular* value in his parents' eyes, irrespective of the others. But even here it is not always possible. Human nature, alas, dictates that each one of us wants to be 'the favourite', 'the best-looking', 'the most gifted' and so on.

Moreover there will always be outsiders to make unhelpful comments within earshot. 'My goodness, isn't your little one pretty' – which to small listening ears is inevitably construed as 'prettier than the others'; or, 'Isn't John clever, you must be so proud of him,' when you have been trying your best not to let him think that he was *more* special – and before you know it, a nasty case of sibling rivalry sets in.

Indeed parents themselves can be so ambitious for their children that they almost encourage extreme competitiveness where it did not exist before. One can just imagine the feelings of the other disciples when the mother of James and John came to ask Jesus if her sons could sit one on the right and one on the left side of his throne when He came into His kingdom ... !

In short, there is a *very* fine dividing line between affirmation and encouragement on the one hand, which are vital, if we are to begin to think positively about our gifts and ourselves, and pushing competitiveness that causes jealousy on the other. Parents need a great deal of loving wisdom if they are to get it right.

The one-talent man

It has always fascinated me that in the parable of the talents it is the one-talent man who stands condemned. This poor creature, who was so desperately aware of how little he had anyway, was to have even this single talent taken away because he did not use it as effectively as the ten-talent man!

For me, loving, or accepting oneself, is the main message of this parable. For the one-talent man was clearly unaccepting of himself, unaccepting of his gift and, above all, full of fear instead of love.

For a long time I personally found this parable hard to stomach. But right here in the parish we have a living testimony to the love and joy that a one-talent person who really accepts herself can give in an elderly lady who has never married and all of whose family have long since died, but whose love and gratitude to the Lord who created her is one of the most incredible testimonies you could ever hope to find. She has never sat around worrying about herself and her lack of gifts, but has given all her time to the love and service of others in the neighbourhood – and to the God she loves with all her heart.

But one thing I know too, without needing to ask, is that she was greatly loved in her own family and made to feel of real value – and the love of God has been able to move in and complete the circle.

Clearly the one talent man in the parable was not! Because he believed he had nothing to give, he hid away out of fear, and buried the only talent he did possess.

Over and over again I have come across people like this in my counselling work. They never volunteer to help out with things that need doing, seldom visit the people around them, and seem to spend their time hiding away and almost apologising for their existence – and all because no one has ever affirmed them as people or encouraged them to look positively at the things they can do, or made them feel loved and wanted.

What can we do?

The trouble is that many such people have their cellar areas extremely well barricaded under a double layer of 'oughts' and 'duties'. The genuine spontaneous interests and talents have long since been buried, along with all the bad feelings and emotions, and if you ask them what their interests are, or what God is saying to them personally, they often *simply do not know*.

Sometimes the key is unlocked by the power of the Holy Spirit, and a creative talent of interest begins to emerge spontaneously from the depths – but at others it can take quite a lot of 'mining' before these personal talents are revealed.

Usually, if they will allow themselves to look, these people do have a distant awareness of something they would like to do deep down. But they are often ashamed of this, perhaps feeling it is unspiritual, or not sufficiently useful to be thought worthwhile. Usually they need a great deal of encouragement to talk about this.

My own mining activities in other people's lives have come up with some fascinatingly diverse interests. One woman had a secret desire to start cultivating an allotment she had been offered, and when I encouraged her it was as if she was suddenly in touch with a wholly new creative and beautiful area of her life. Watching the plants grow and being involved with the wonderful healing therapy that exists in nature turned out to be the key to many other creative talents that had lain buried for years.

Then there was the clergyman who had a great longing to learn ballroom dancing, but had never had the courage to tell his wife! When he eventually did she was surprised, but more than ready to go along with this. This was a physical and emotional tension release for a man who had not only kept his fears and problems bottled up within the muscular control line I mentioned earlier, but had also lived so much in his very brilliant mind, that he was almost completely out of touch with his body and his feelings.

Dancing and physical activity of many different kinds have proved to be a great release for people like this, as

indeed have music or painting and all the other creative
gifts.

It concerns me greatly how narrow many of us have
allowed our Christian lives to become, in contrast to the
amazing creativity that Almighty God has given us in the
universe. We do not ask, 'Of what *use* is a sunset, or the
extraordinary beauty of the heavens on a clear starlit
night?' and yet many of us narrow down our lives to things
that are apparently purely 'useful' and 'productive', as if
we imagined that God was actually asking us to do this.
And in this self-imposed destruction of creativity, we often
lose sight of the many talents He has given us to use and to
enjoy – the very things that will help us find out who we
are.

Holding up the mirror ...

I actually believe it is quite difficult to help ourselves with
finding our own value and identity, and we may need the
help and insight of friends to hold up a mirror for us – to
show us what we are really like, and the gifts and attributes
that they value in us.

For myself I have several really close friends that I can
talk things through with – as they do with me. I know that
I can trust them absolutely to tell me what they really
think. And in the beginning, when I was just setting out
on the journey of finding myself and the particular talents
that God had given me, they had to encourage me a great
deal. Years of unhappiness had produced a deep sense of
inadequacy in certain areas, and there were a lot of things I
could not seem to 'hear', however many times I was told!

We had a really classic case of this once in a counselling
group that I was leading. The exercise was to go round the
small circle of people, who by this time had got to know
each other pretty well, and to say how we experienced the
other members of the group. One of our number was a
young veterinary surgeon that everyone liked. But as we

went round the group, with one person after another
saying how much they had valued his support, his insight
and just the warmth of his presence, he was deaf to every
word, almost angrily denying that any of this could
possibly be true. Finally someone came up with a very
minor thing about him that they did not like, and he leapt
onto this with tremendous enthusiasm, agreeing absolutely! Years of parental criticism had convinced him that
there was nothing good that could possibly be said about
him – he was a failure and there was an end to it!
Eventually, I am happy to say, the love and affirmation of
people in the group got through – but it was a long hard
battle.

The gift of encouragement

It is a plain fact that we *all* need encouragement and
affirmation both of our gifts and ourselves. And this even
includes the ten-talent people who seem to have no needs
that we can see! In fact, as I know from my work, there are
many well-known Christian leaders who desperately need
love and support, but who are often deprived of this –
either because people think they do not need it, or because
their status makes them feel a threat to others. Everyone
needs loving supportive friends, and even becoming a
national figure in any sphere does not lessen this need – if
anything it is greatly increased!

The ministry of encouragement is one of the most
precious in the book, and one that all of us can benefit
from. One friend of mine who possesses this gift prayed for
it very specifically, and it was certainly not a natural
attribute. She is in fact a very able analytical kind of person
who is capable of being extremely critical. In asking for
this gift she was able to turn something that might
otherwise have been very destructive into something
wonderfully creative.

But this sort of activity certainly sorts the sheep out from the goats in terms of self acceptance! And if you are one of those people who is still questioning whether a book with such a title should ever have been written, then this is your own personal piece of litmus paper.

Are you sufficiently secure in your own identity and sense of self worth that you can go out to someone who seems to be more gifted, or better known than yourself and seek for ways in which you can help or support him, *without* feeling inadequate, resentful, or just plain unwilling?

The man who has learnt to accept himself and his talents *as they are* is the only one who will honestly be able to go out in love to other people in this way. In other words he will truly be able to love others as he loves himself.

If he is still wishing that he was as good as the other person, or that his own talents had been recognised, then he will be quite unable to do this with any sincerity. Just as those who have been given love are more able to give it to others, so those who are secure in the knowledge of their own gifts and talents will be able to affirm those of other people without feeling threatened or inadequate.

We have to so build up the confidence and self acceptance of those who feel that they have nothing to give, that real love becomes a possibility for them, and this will require some honest heart-to-heart communication about the *real*, and not the pretend 'front-room' situation.

When he has first faced up to the question, 'How much are this person's looks, gifts, abilities and insights making me feel inadequate or threatened?' then and only then will he be able to ask, 'In what way can I help him by giving him my support and encouragement?'

Once a man knows his own value and identity and begins to actually *experience* the love of God and of others then for the *first time* he is able to forget about himself!

7

Real-Life Love

Some years ago now a minister who had just begun to
work in the field of counselling used to spend a short time
praying for someone's release and healing, and then go
away leaving that person with the assumption that they
were now 'better'. Certainly the person felt better, after
being prayed with and listened to, but his problems had
not all gone away. For a start this was just the tip of the
iceberg and there were probably a great many more hours
that would still be needed in the future. I usually describe
it as being like layers of wallpaper on an old and badly
papered wall – they have to come off one at a time before
we can get down to the real plaster, 'the real me'. And
when this is done within the love of God He is very gentle
with us, knowing perfectly well that if the memories are
very bad then we cannot possibly cope with this at one
sitting.

But, in addition to the actual feelings and problems,
whatever they might be, the individual himself is still the
adult product of many years of neglect and lack of loving
support which no *one* session could possibly heal. A cut or
a wound that was caused in an instant may very well heal
over in a few days or weeks. But hurts and rejections that
have taken place over a lifetime, often at the hands of many
different human beings, cannot possibly be healed in such
a way. Even if the root cause has been worked out or dealt
with, we are still left with a badly damaged and battered

personality who may need many years of loving support and understanding.

There are *no* quick and easy short cuts in the world of helping people! Jesus Himself spent three solid years being with, supporting and teaching the disciples before He sent them out. And we ourselves look after our children for many years before we entrust them to the outside world.

It has always fascinated me how *long* some Bible characters took in the making. Just take a look at how many years God took in dealing with Moses or Joseph, and even Paul after his experience on the Damascus road. So why are we always in such a hurry? I am afraid I strongly suspect that, because loving and helping people is such a time-consuming business, we mostly prefer the quick, easy, 'purely spiritual' way out!

Isn't it curious that Jesus spent such a large part of His ministry building up and teaching just twelve disciples – one of whom was such a dead loss anyway! Was He just teaching them and living out the life of God before them, or was He helping each one of them individually to find love and wholeness, and to recognise the gifts that they had been given?

There was a particularly telling scene in the musical show *Godspell* where the character of Jesus goes round the circle of His followers acting out the relationship He had with each one of them personally – and each one was completely *different*! One can just imagine the many hours out on the mountainside or in the olive groves that He had spent talking alone with that particular man or woman – helping, encouraging, affirming and understanding them. He knew all about them – their weaknesses and their fears, their strengths and their hopes, and He gave them all His attention in those few precious hours alone. Are our needs any different?

Of course the glib easy way is to spiritualise it all. If a new believer spends sufficient time in Bible study and prayer then this alone will make up the deficit – in other words God will do it all! But is that our experience, and is it even what Jesus told His followers to do when He left them? Surely the command was to 'love each other as I have loved you.'

For all God's love and inner healing that I have experienced it is still true that the greatest day-to-day strength and support that I have known has come from other Christian friends and their love. If you like, it is an outward and visible sign of an inward and invisible truth – that I know I am loved by God, because I am loved by others in His name.

Inasmuch as you did it to the least of these my brethren you did it unto me ...

Of course as the years go by our relationship with God will deepen and our spiritual lives will grow, but this I believe is supposed to happen *alongside* our relationship with our fellow Christians. Indeed, the one feeds and enables the other.

I Corinthians Chapter 13 supports this theory at great length when we are told:

> If I speak in the tongues of men and of angels, but have not love, I am only a resounding gong or a clanging cymbal. If I have the gift of prophecy and can fathom all mysteries and all knowledge and if I have a faith that can move mountains, but have not love, I am nothing. If I give all I possess to the poor and surrender my body to the flames, but have not love, I gain nothing. (NIV)

By any standards these are awesome words, and sometimes I wonder how well we have 'heard' them!

Often I meet people who come to me or to others for counselling and help, but what they really need more than anything is genuine ongoing love, freely given. But so often we become 'weary in well doing ...'

The broken reeds who inevitably exist round the fringes of our churches have seemingly a bottomless pit of need for love. However 'unlovely' some of them may be, we have been commanded to love them, and indeed who else will? Doctors are too busy, social workers have many more cases on their hands, and they come to us in the desperate hope that we can help.

Let's be realistic and admit that mixing with the unpopular, the way-out or the known sinners or addicts can be a very threatening experience for some of us. If we are at all unsure of ourselves or our status then we may feel 'contaminated' or 'affected' in some way or other. What would people (especially our fellow Christians) think? Ought I to give him the book of rules first, so he knows I don't approve? Could I be known as *his* friend?

However, these and many other similar feelings say nothing about real love and acceptance and nothing about the nature of God either. They are easily recognisable as what psychologists call 'parent tapes', and you may know some of them from your own experience. 'Don't you play with that boy over the road, his parents are not nice.' 'We only want you to mix with the best people' – and so on. It may sound silly, but until and unless we take a long hard look at some of the instructions our parents and authority figures have given us, in the light of God's true love as seen in the Bible, it is often really difficult to distinguish the one from the other, so before we can really love and help these people we often have to be helped ourselves, and to be strong enough to cope with the demands that are made on us. Or, to quote Dr Dobson, 'Love must be tough.'

Sarah lived on my doorstep, haunted the kitchen, and always managed to telephone just as I was going out. Moreover, she unfailingly produced her most pressing problem that I simply 'had to' help her with just as she was supposed to be going ...

Anyone who has anything to do with helping people will recognise this character instantly! And what eventually happens to her?

To begin with I will accept her coming and try my best to help with the unending series of problems, but as the hours turn to days and the days to months, I get positively neurotic at the sound of her voice. After a month or two my feelings towards her can no longer even loosely be classified as 'love', since they more naturally resemble outright resentment! How can she possibly do this to me? Surely she must know that I can't cope with it, and anyway however much help I give her she never seems to get any better ...

Finally the chances are that my tolerance will snap, and I will tell her exactly what I feel in total exasperation – thus undoing all the good that might previously have been done! And probably I will lay all the blame at her door, whilst continuing to feel uneasily guilty myself ...

In actual fact the *real* problem is that *I* have not got to grips with my *own* needs! And even if I do actually know what they are, I will probably never have given myself permission to have such needs! After all it doesn't seem very Christian ...

I could have dealt with Sarah far more lovingly and far more effectively if I had been able to say to her kindly from the beginning, 'Look, I really want to help you, but I honestly can't cope with you soaking up this much of my time. I have a lot of other things to do, and anyway I am the sort of person who needs a bit more space.' That is to say, *I* am taking the responsibility for how *I* feel, and not just blaming her.

I will then sort out the guidelines for the time I can lovingly give her and *stick to this*! I might say something like this: 'Let's make a regular time when you can come round, perhaps twice a week for an hour at a time [or whatever you can realistically cope with]. And when you come round, tell me *right away* what is really bothering you, and then we will have time to deal with this instead of it just coming up as you are about to leave, and it's too late.'

Once Sarah knows that these are my perimeters – though I may have to be fairly tough to start with – then she will be motivated to help me in return. In fact she will eventually be quite proud of the fact that she *can* cope, and that she is lovingly helping *me* in this way. In other words I am helping her to grow up and take responsibility for her own life, but at the same time giving her the regular ongoing structured support she needs.

Later on I will be able to extend the gap, so that it becomes once a week or whatever. In the meantime she is discovering to her delight that she *can* cope, without needing to cling to me like a drowning child.

In all our dealings with other people it is vital that we are honest about our own needs, without feeling guilty about this. It is all a part of telling people 'who we are' and how they can relate to us. Of course there will be times when we have to endure beyond the limits of what we would humanly choose to do – perhaps in a crisis, or in some situation in which the Lord has made the need very clear to us. But as a general rule, real-life love will only grow in a relationship when we are honest about our own needs and limitations, without just assuming that the other person will know what they are – because he very seldom does!

Another obvious casualty in the area of lovingly helping others around us will be our own homes. The number of clergy families, for instance, that have paid the full price for this neglect of personal needs is quite frightening.

While the minister has no doubt been a significant help to those who have come to him, his own family have often grown up to resent the way that his love has been taken away from them to give to others. In the end they have often directed this resentment onto God, and thereby lost their faith. And one is driven to ask, 'Was it worth the sacrifice?'

When I first got involved in the field of helping people, I soon found that there were not enough hours in the day to see those who wanted to come. I never had a moment to myself, or a drop of energy left to give enough love and care to my own husband and children when they came home. Happily, with the help of others I was quick to realise the situation, and set myself realistic limits for what I could cope with, and just how much God expected me to give.

Unfortunately there is another syndrome that gets in the way here, which I will call 'Neurotic Need Meeters Inc.'! Many 'helpers' come into this category, and we do well to put our finger on our own pulses if we are in any way involved.

Usually such people are the older brothers and sisters, or those who have been expected to help and cope in their childhood homes as a matter of duty. 'Look after little Johnny for me while I go out,' 'I need you to help with the younger ones,' 'You are the one I rely on' – and so on. Doubtless these words will ring many bells from the past. But the trouble is that unless we are very careful, this automatic-pilot 'duty' tape simply carries on rolling – at the expense of our homes and families, and also of our own needs – often to a disastrous extent.

Such a person will not know 'who he is' either, because he exists only to help others – he has no other identity of his own. He is a compulsive 'need meeter', and usually feels that his only justification for being around is as a 'helper', just as it was at home.

Doubtless at this point many readers will be feeling fairly uptight – but let me explain the pitfalls.

I have known this situation well, from the inside, and it can be very draining. Like the rest of us, the need meeter also needs to see that he is loved and wanted for himself, and not just because he is able to help others, although this will almost certainly remain one of his primary ministries.

There will be times when he also has needs, and when he should be taking time off for relaxation and refreshment. If he only sees himself as a 'helper' he may well find this very difficult. Sometimes it will be necessary for friends to come alongside with loving support to ease the burden as well as to show him that they value him as an individual in his own right, otherwise this man may continue to ignore his own needs and those of his family, and there is also a very great danger that he will not be any *lasting* help to the people he is trying to help either!

If his only reason for being around is to help others, then he will probably find it very difficult to let these people go when they actually need to be pushed out. The feeling of having people dependent on him is naturally quite rewarding and also very familiar – it is always nice to be needed. But alas, certain people, like Sarah, have an uncanny knack for searching out these weak spots.

While the Sarahs of this world need to be encouraged, after sufficient help and support has been given, to grow up and move out as adults – drawing their main strength from God and from other Christians in the fellowship – they would naturally prefer to remain as clinging children, soaking every last drop of milk from the compulsive need-meeting parent. And if the parent is not perceptive and strong enough to move her roots gradually out of his own back yard into the wider Christian field where they belong, he is effectively failing to help her grow up and take responsibility for herself at all. Alas, his own needs to be needed are too strong and have never been recognised.

Real-life love never includes allowing ourselves to be doormats. And if, as we expect within a Christian fellowship, people want to love and help us in return, then how can they do this unless they know what our needs are?

8

Real-Life Fellowship

In every chapter so far I have spoken about the need to really help and support one another in the name of Christ, with the love that we have been given. And indeed, with this aim in view, it would be hard to imagine any group of people meeting together with greater potential than a Christian fellowship. But I wonder how often this is really recognised, or put to its maximum use.

Sometimes you can go to a group where the atmosphere is almost rarefied – as if the people present didn't need the air that other people breathe at all! There *are* times, of course, when we are genuinely lost in wonder, love and praise for our Creator, when this can be a very real atmosphere, where we are indeed treading on holy ground. But for most of our lives we are ordinary human beings, and it seems to me that we must be very careful not to separate God from our situation. It is not *necessary* for every sentence to have a sort of 'holy' or biblical aura to it, preferably backed up by chapter and verse, or worse still to be made to feel that you cannot question or disagree with anything that has been said.

Whether our fellowship takes the form of Bible study, discussion or prayer, the main aim must surely be to bring the people present closer to God and to one another. But if we are going to help the people who come to grow in the knowledge and love of God, then we have got to help them from where they *really are*, and not from the 'front-room' position which they may well be feeling that they must maintain. To do this requires a deep awareness and sensitivity on the part of the leaders, which it is vital that we cultivate.

While others affirm how rewarding their Christian experience is, does the person who's feeling anything but strong in his faith keep quiet, all the while feeling very inadequate because quite frankly his quiet times are not nearly so 'easy' or 'heavenly' at all? Does he agree because he feels he ought to, and is not too sure what is expected of him in this group anyhow? Or does he leave with some apparently valid excuse, but in reality because there is no genuine food or sustenance to be found here?

All of these situations are about unreality and the impossiblity of sharing what is really going on in my 'God life' with others. I cannot say 'who I am' or 'what I feel', because instinctively I sense that the reality will not be acceptable. It may say something about my uncertainty as a person, but it also says a great deal about the usefulness of the group to which I belong!

Several years ago now, when I first became aware of this whole syndrome through my counselling work, I began to see our daytime fellowship group for what it really was – and decided there had to be a sort of make-or-break exercise! Metaphorically it was up to me to lay myself on the line. First of all I shared with them quite a lot about my own Christian life – the problems, the doubts and the needs I sometimes had, and which incidentally they had imagined *I never* experienced. And then I owned up to the fact that I had not at any time felt a great deal of support or real fellowship with them!

After the stunned silence, I then invited them to share with the rest of us something of themselves, and what their needs and expectations from the group were too.

The results might be an object lesson for all of us! The atmosphere lightened immediately, and people found themselves sharing things that they had obviously carried around with them for years. One woman said that she had many times come to the group and gone away with problems she had never dared to share – because she felt that no one else there would understand, and that they would reject her if she owned up to these! Another admitted that she had often come along without understanding a great deal of what we were talking about, but desperately needing help and friendship. Yet another said that spiritually some of us seemed so far ahead of her that she felt that she could never catch up or dare to ask for help.

From that day on the group began to grow and develop into a *real* fellowship, and people went away with a completely new door opened in their lives. Instead of being stuck in their faith, as some had been, coming along out of duty, they were now able to talk quite openly about any problems they had. Suddenly we had been set free to share our *real* experiences, both good and bad, with one another, and so find the support that all of us needed. And of course our prayer times were now about the needs and concerns that really worried us deep down, thus openly inviting God to work in the cellar areas of all of our lives.

I will also be honest and tell you that one woman left for a few months, because being truly 'English' she felt that she could never share the realities of her life and faith in this way. We simply accepted that this was what she felt, staying close to her as a friend – and it wasn't long before she was back with us again. Indeed if I look back now I can date her growth as a really loving genuine Christian from that time.

With any group of Christians meeting together it is absolutely essential for us to be honest with one another. Without this there will never be any real growth, but simply an increase in the spiritual icing on top of the cake! We have been told to love one another and to share one another's burdens and there is *no way* we can possibly do this unless we are going to know and accept one another as real people.

But is it 'Christian' ... ?

I am sure that some people reading this will already be saying to themselves that this sort of fellowship does not belong in a Bible study or Christian meeting. After all, we will only be there to increase our knowledge of God and this has nothing to do with feelings – indeed this might be a dangerous side track!

The problem with 'head knowledge' is that, if we don't watch out, this is exactly where the knowledge goes – and no further! I know any number of Christians who could make rings round people in quoting chapter and verse, not to mention all the books they have read and doctrines they could expound – but very many times I am aware that this is not having a great deal of effect either on their *lives* or on the peace and joy that they actually *experience*.

But supposing such a man were in a group of people, like himself, who were prepared to risk talking about the doubts and problems they do sometimes experience, and to explore those areas in depth, really seeking to help one another?

We have been in a number of such groups over the past few years and the help and support to all those present – at least all who were prepared to be absolutely honest – has been quite remarkable.

One group was composed largely of new or fringe believers who thought quite deeply about things, and still had a lot of questions and problems to air. They felt totally free to do this within the safety of the group. No one said, 'Oh you shouldn't query that,' or gave any indication of disapproval, and the whole group was a very stimulating and mind-stretching affair for all of us – though a few of the 'older' Christians had problems to begin with about whether or not it was 'okay' to range so far away from the Bible passage we were studying at the time. But when people had problems and queries we were able to deal with them at source, rather than gloss over them in the name of keeping to the text! The end result of this particular group was a whole lot of people much more strongly rooted and grounded in their faith, and free to be themselves in the knowledge and love of God and of each other.

Perhaps one should add a caveat here, since there are certain individuals who cannot seem to avoid bringing the whole group back time and again to their own personal problems. Needless to say, this is of no great benefit to the group as a whole, or in actual fact to the individual concerned, since he keeps on coming back to it! If the problem is really of an emotional or psychological nature, then it would be much better dealt with either by a counsellor, or within the safety of a growth group constituted for the purpose. It is, however, important that the problem *is* dealt with – and that this particular person's need for attention is both recognised and contained.

Another group that we have been involved with is one that I am convinced is very badly needed right across the Christian church – and that is the neighbourhood peer group.

In our case this has been just four couples, all involved in leadership positions and carrying a lot of responsibility in the area. We meet across parish boundaries and do not see each other all that often – perhaps five or six times a year. But when we have got together, we have found the fellowship the most enormous strength and support. Over the last few years we have discussed almost every 'hairy' issue that has faced us personally as Christians, or in the wider church – issues that it would be difficult for us to share in any other context.

Moreover we have supported one another through the personal problems that have faced each one of us during that time – a doctor coping with the death of a patient very close to him, a clergyman facing problems with dissension

in his parish, and ourselves going through a takeover
situation followed by redundancy – not to mention all the
usual family problems! Whatever the situation, we have
known real love and support, and a rock-solid base of
fellowship that was totally real – with no need of pretence
or of keeping up a good 'front'! How many Christian
leaders I know who could benefit from this kind of group,
and how few have experienced the blessings it can bring!

Personally I believe that peer groups of every kind are a
necessity and not an optional extra. Most churches have
young people's fellowships and wives' groups, but what
about a group for men only, where they can feel free to
share issues from work and family, in an atmosphere
where they can find support and understanding. Wherever
such groups have started up they have proved a real
blessing to the men concerned, who had usually felt that
they could not share such issues in a mixed group and been
unable to grow as a result. Similarly many fellowship
groups for the unemployed are fast becoming an essential
part of church life, not to mention a very practical way of
providing help and caring for others in the area.

A different kind of fellowship and one that is vital for
the purpose of helping people to find their own value and
sense of self worth, is the short-term 'growth group'.
Usually this needs to be quite small – about eight or ten
people, including one or two with some experience of
counselling. The main purpose of this kind of group is to
help one another grow as real flesh-and-blood Christians.

In such a group I personally have been helped more
than I can say by people telling me face to face what I really
mean to them – and there will be many many people in our
midst who need this kind of affirmation. I have also been
helped by people being honest enough to tell me that
sometimes I make them feel inadequate, or threaten them
in some way. It is far better to know from the person in
question than to feel that something is wrong and not
know what the trouble really is. This to me is 'speaking

the truth in love', and it enables us to take a completely new look at the relationship and to see what is really wrong. It may even simply be that we remind them of someone from the past that they could not cope with, or something that they imagine we are thinking about them. But honestly, when you know even as little as I do about this then there is no way you can be really sure what is going on in a relationship unless you are prepared to be absolutely honest with one another – 'armour' off!

As a result of many such groups over a long period of time, the level of real love and fellowship in our church has deepened remarkably, and complete strangers often comment on this the moment they walk in at the door.

In such a group the supernatural gifts can also be of great value. When we do not know or cannot see with human eyes what deep unhappiness is lurking in someone's cellar, then very often a 'picture' or a word of knowledge from the Lord will provide the necessary clue, thus opening doors that have remained padlocked for years.

In all such groups we will be able to pray for one another and for our *real* needs with much greater impact. The healing power that exists within a loving real-life fellowship such as this needs seeing to be believed! Through this channel I and many others have come to know what it is to love one another in deed and in truth – and to grow on that rock-solid foundation.

9

On the Bottom Rung

While I have talked in general terms about ways in which we can help ourselves and others to discover our identity before God and to recognise our own value as individuals, there is obviously a deeper level of help to which I have only referred in passing. Once we get down to this level, whether we are talking about healing of the memories or psychotherapy, about the removal of oppressive spirits or working out deeply ingrained emotional problems, this is bound to involve finding a source of more experienced or professional help.[1] Indeed even writing generally on this subject alone would take a whole book, and many such have already been written. So let me give just a few instances of the kind of problems that can be dealt with in this way, and the controversies that unfortunately exist over this whole area in the Christian world.

Whilst I and many others have received help from several of the ministries listed, not all those involved in counselling work would go along with this! The tendency is to hug our own particular corners.

Counsellors involved in the more practical psychological outworking of deep emotional hurts and fears sometimes treat the spiritual healing ministries a little cynically. Those with healing gifts quite often regard psychologically based counselling with some suspicion, seeing it as rather unspiritual or unnecessary.

[1]See list in appendix on page 110

Just like the gifts within the body I believe that God has given us this wide variety of healing methods to be *used*. And those I know who have found the greatest blessing in wholeness are the ones who have been open to whatever ministry God wanted them to use.

For example, after I had worked out most of the deeper feelings of bereavement and anger lurking in my cellar area I felt infinitely freer and more relaxed as a person – so much so that people who had not seen me for a while would comment on how much I had visibly changed. *But* many of these areas still hurt. The healing love of God had not been poured into the wounds, and they remained open for anyone to stamp on – however unwittingly. And it was only after someone had prayed with me for the actual healing of the memories that I actually found real lasting freedom, where the hurts had ceased to be open wounds but merely scars.

The corollary is also true. I have met many people through my counselling who have been prayed with for inner healing, but who are still a seething mass of destructive emotions which have never been allowed to see the light of day – anger, frustration, fear and tears to mention just a few. If applying the plaster of spiritual healing to these wounds does not remove the feelings, then it will be necessary to remove the plaster and let out all the pus first, before any lasting healing can take place.

Another very controversial area is that of the removal of oppressive spirits – which I must confess that I used to ridicule myself until a few years ago! I had met people who 'saw' spirits under every bush, and who most conveniently blamed every bad thought of anger or lust on to a spirit of that name – which seemed to me a very easy way out!

Since that time, though I still believe that much of this kind of thing is questionable, I have come to see that there *are* areas of spiritual oppression that need to be looked at, at very least when all else fails. Moreover these things are very adept at hiding under perfectly logical and predictable psychological symptoms. For example someone who has been left alone feeling unloved and rejected most of his childhood will obviously find it extremely difficult to make relationships or to feel that anyone cares about him. But if even after many months of loving care and support he *still* feels unloved, unwanted and unaccepted, one might well start to look a bit further for something like a spirit of rejection.

I had always thought that such occult interference would have to involve some sort of dabbling or active interest in that field, but many cases have come to light which show that if a child gets defencelessly low and alone, he can be 'oppressed' by such spirits even though they may not actually have a grip on him physically – and as a result he will never get significantly better unless something is done about this.

I now find myself looking much more closely at the gospel narrative to see how many times Jesus actually stopped to remove yet another spirit, which no one else could identify.

Which brings me to another very important point. How essential it is that someone in our fellowship should possess the gift of discernment to be able to see through the superficial symptoms with the X-ray eyes of God Himself.

Too often in my opinion we have seen the frantic casting out of spirits when the person in question is obviously suffering from perfectly normal psychological and emotional symptoms which just need loving care and treatment. Correspondingly a man has been treated for the symptoms alone, with no reference or thought given to whether or not there is some deeper evil lurking in the background.

Once more we come back to the gifts within the body, and the very real need to have people trained and gifted in *all* these different areas, if we are to provide a comprehensive ministry to the people who come for help.

The most helpful experience I have personally had was

to go back through the years to the really painful and bitter memories, and even back to birth itself. With the help of someone ministering in His name, I have experienced Christ there actually with me at those moments, and known both what He wanted to say to me, and also how He felt about the things that happened. It is difficult to describe the experience but I can only say that it was very deeply moving and extremely real. Now I have genuinely been able to leave these experiences behind me, knowing that God has healed me once and for all, and that they can never affect me in the same way again.

So, when we are down on the bottom rung of our cellar areas it is not necessarily enough for us just to try to face these deeper emotions and fears with the help of a friend, or even in a secure accepting group. They will need the individual help and insight of a trained counsellor.

As I said in an earlier chapter, it is our deep inner feelings that make up our real selves, but it may be difficult if not impossible to recognise these feelings. We will have spent so long denying them and pretending that they don't exist, that in all probability we will be quite unable to find the key by ourselves.

Moreover, since the reason we barricaded these feelings away in the first place was that we could not cope with them, or that they were 'unacceptable', it is even *more* vital that when we are on the bottom rung we explore these cellar areas in good company – or with the genuine loving support of someone trained to help who will not let us down again.

Jennifer came to me in a very angry state, because her boss at work was really pushing her around, and she could neither cope with this nor tell him how she felt. But as I listened it seemed to me that she was definitely over-reacting, and that there must be something else behind this. I asked her to have an imaginary conversation with the boss in front of me, and it became clear that many of the things that she said were 'projections' from her own cellar area. Even the words that she used were child words, and it was clear that her boss represented her parents in some way. Although she was an able and gifted woman, she seemed almost paralytically incapable of coping with any kind of authority. It seemed to reduce her to childhood at the turn of a switch, thus preventing her from standing up for herself, or saying what she really thought.

The situation with her boss was my only clue, and so I asked her how she would deal with him – offering her a tennis racket or a pillow to beat. She chose the pillow and set to work without the necessity of much encouragement from me!

Barely thirty seconds into the exercise, and, as I had suspected, the boss had suddenly 'become' her father and mother, and all kinds of memories and fears from her cellar area came charging back into her conscious mind, first with anger and then with tears. But as she worked this out, and came to the end of the exercise in sheer exhaustion, it was not difficult to see the change in her. As she stood up, she suddenly seemed taller and more confident. 'It's a funny thing,' she said, 'but somehow they seem to have come down to size. I'm not a child any more – in fact now I feel I can cope with them all without being afraid.'

I am quite sure that many Christians reading this will feel alarmed at the thought of allowing anyone to express their feelings in this way. But firstly this kind of working out is often the only way of releasing the real person underneath the heap of rubble, and secondly it harms no one, since all the feelings are released in a purely clinical environment. Indeed this will actually protect others around us from sporadic and unreasonable outbursts, which are bound to occur when such cellar feelings have not been dealt with.

The feelings are directed at past memories, and in this way it enables us to finally bury the past and move freely into the future.

Jennifer returned to work no longer afraid of her boss, but able to speak up when she needed to. He in turn came to respect her opinion and trust her as the adult she had become, instead of the sullen cringing child.

At home she was suddenly able to talk out many of the hurtful memories with her parents. Naturally to begin with this was quite a shock to them, after so many years of compliance. But before many months had passed their relationship was better than it had ever been. Instead of being afraid of them she was able to understand and help them, with love instead of resentment. She was now free to be herself.

There are, of course, many other ways of getting rid of the hurts and memories that bind us. For example it is a known fact that whilst the body remembers, the mind often forgets, and quite often a persistent pain unrelated to anything physical, tension in the back or even certain smells or sounds can unlock the gates that barricade the past. Through some form of therapy, we are able to go back 'through' that feeling to the memories it evokes to actually relive that situation in order to finally get free of this once and for all.

As I said earlier, if we are doing this under the Lordship of Christ and using His healing gifts, then the layers of wallpaper that have hidden the person for so long will only be removed gently and in God's good time – which quite frankly is necessary if we are going to cope with the changes both in our everyday lives and in our relationships.

Quite often reliving past hurtful memories can occur spontaneously during prayer counselling, or even alone in our own homes under the power of the Holy Spirit. There is nothing sinister about any of this. It is necessary because over a period of time we have so pushed our feelings down into the cellar area that we have become bottled up under this heap of hidden emotion, with no freedom to respond with any degree of spontaneity to people and events around us. Nearly always it is something hidden in this memory bank which prevents us moving with any degree of freedom into the future – to find the abundant life that Jesus promised us.

10

A Complete Ministry in the Church?

If we are going to help people in our churches to find their real identities and the gifts that God has given them we will have to take a long hard look at how to achieve this.

In all honesty we must admit that many Christians have not yet discovered the wells of abundant life that Jesus came to bring. And any thinking person must realise that this situation may get worse rather than better as the years go by, with so many broken homes, so many single parents struggling desperately to cope and children feeling rejected and abandoned – tossed like so much unwanted flotsam on the waves of bitterness between separated parents. We are in fact breeding a whole new generation of emotional cripples on a scale that has never been known before. And this is not including the millions of unemployed in the world who feel that they have no value because their only identity is in the job that they can no longer find.

Certainly we want to tell them the good news of the gospel, and to help them to find eternal life – but we are told that eternal life begins *now*. It is a completely new quality of life with rivers of living water springing fresh each day. We have to help the men and women in our churches to *find* the true freedom that Jesus died to bring us – and not just to talk about it! Such an exercise will of course be very costly in terms of time and ministry.

Recognising the needs

Quite a few churches have already recognised the need that
lies all around them. One well-known church in our area
has now one full-time and one part-time counsellor on its
staff, while the church fellowships are organised in such a
way as to be small enough for people to share the needs
and problems that they have.

It seems to me that in today's world the church is having
the greatest impact where it is really reaching through to
people's needs – with a faith that is live and relevant to
their everyday experience. It is our *love* that will get
through to them far more effectively than artificial self-
conscious evangelism. Although obviously I don't mean
that we should not talk in everyday language about the
faith that we hold.

A couple who went along to a Marriage Encounter
weekend, where they were greatly helped in their
relationship by the Christians who led the sessions, had
scarcely ever darkened the door of any church. But from
this weekend they were so impressed with the love that
they were shown that they immediately wanted to know
what motivated these people.

Again, the many groups that are operating all round the
country to help and support the unemployed are
providing a lot of light in an area of real darkness.
Inevitably the people who are drawn into these groups
will see something of the love of God at work – but it must
be genuine wholehearted love, no strings attached. Not I
will love you '*if* you become a Christian', 'join our
church', or whatever. Often outsiders have had such bad
experiences of RE lessons and the image that some
Christians present that they will want to test the reality of
our love.

But what can we do to help the people *in* our churches
grow and change and get free of the chains from the past
that bind them?

First of all we must try to see the situation as it *is*, and not attempt to spiritualise it away. We have in our congregations people who have come into a real relationship with God, but who need help and encouragement within a secure environment to find themselves and their value in God's eyes.

Help must start at the top

Often the only way that they will risk this is if the minister himself or the group leader takes the first step - perhaps by admitting that he is vulnerable, that he has needs and problems too! If *he* is prepared to share with me what he is really like - i.e. something of himself - then it might be safe for me to risk this too ... I actually think that one of the reasons that churches are not coping adequately with this problem is that ministers and elders have not *themselves* received sufficient help in this field. And as I have said it is very difficult to help others unless you have first been helped yourself.

Every strand of the church, from the Established Theological Training Colleges, to the House Church 'authority' teaching, not to mention the priestly 'status' of the more Catholic ministries, tends towards the same inherent danger - that of putting its leadership on a pedestal, and often expecting the impossible of them as a result. Many ministers I know have actually been told never to share their needs with others in the church, and the burdens they have carried - often quite unnecessarily - have been colossal.

It was the discovery of such a situation that led Dr Frank Lake to put together the best of current psychology, using Jesus as the model - now known as Clinical Theology. To his horror, on visiting the local mental home, he found a *whole ward* of clerical patients who had been unable to cope with their parishes' expectations of them, and unwilling to verbalise any needs or weaknesses for fear of

rejection. Needless to say this left Dr Lake wondering what
we had misunderstood about the Christian message that
apparently left so many people broken and unable to cope!

I do not myself find the instructions anywhere in the
New Testament that our leaders are meant to be elevated to
some kind of pedestal, without adequate support and
burden sharing – and often six foot above contradiction!
Look at the number of times that Paul talks about his need
of support and fellowship from Timothy and others in
those young churches, and how much he misses them
when they are away. Even our Lord Himself seems
deliberately to have gone out of His way to choose Peter,
James and John to be His own personal support group.
And if the Son of God Himself needed this kind of human
strengthening, *how much more do our leaders in the
church need this today?*

Nearly all the most successful ministries within the
church today seem to have their own special prayer and
support group, and this is as true for Billy Graham and the
Archbishop of Canterbury as it was for David Watson and
is for many lesser known people. There are one or two
others known to me who would very much like to do this,
but have never been able to take the first step, or to find the
people that they felt they could really trust. Perhaps this
will show some of us in the congregation a very practical
way in which we could offer to help?

The desperate need for trained people

Once we get down to the cellar area and the bottom rung of
the ladder, then we are in a very different territory and we
shall need people trained and able to really help with all
these deeper problems. There is such a need for
counselling of this kind that many other organisations
have cashed in on this account where the church should
have been playing its part. For example Scientologists
actively go around looking for people in need, whilst

using some of the more advanced psychological techniques to further their sinister cause.

Another so-called fellowship, known as the Earmark Trust, used similar techniques to draw in people needing counselling help. The people who went were like lambs to the slaughter, trusting the 'spiritual' mask that the leader was wearing. When he died it was revealed that a great many people had given him all their life savings, and that they had been put into groups that were actively and deliberately destructive of personality whilst purporting to be 'Christian'.

The Moonies and many of the other cults that exist in today's broken society are using the same kind of techniques. They have recognised the vast numbers of needy young people around today, together with the degree of real spiritual hunger that exists, and are using their brokenness to manipulate and destroy them. Indeed many parents rightly live in fear of their children ever getting involved in this way, because they know that it is extremely unlikely that they will ever see them again ...

But *why* hasn't the church stepped in to take up its responsibility in facing up to this need? And how long is it going to take for us to wake up?

Many years ago now, when our previous vicar realised how vital this kind of ministry was, he did everything in his power to get all the leaders in the church on to a Christian counselling course. By the time he left, even the hundred-strong Youth Group was regularly divided into small caring 'support groups' where young people were able to share the many problems and fears that they inevitably had.

Just as people in the past have left the churches searching for renewal and the reality of spiritual experience that they could not find in seemingly irrelevant services, so now, if the deeper needs within our churches are not recognised and met, we can confidently expect the same exodus to take place. Worse than that, we shall truly be ignoring the needs of many thousands in the community around us.

11

Freedom To Be Myself

If we have been completely honest about what lurks in the cellars of our lives, we will have faced not only our hurts and bitter experiences, but also our more tenacious and well-hidden sins. Although we will undoubtedly still have a long way to go on the journey of becoming more like Christ, our lives will now be open to the the light and power of His Holy Spirit. There will no longer be any need for the cover-up camouflage we have used previously, but instead, the spontaneous fruits of the Spirit will start to emerge from deep inside our very being, along with opinions and beliefs that are *our own*, not second-hand. Any doubts that we have had about the reality of our faith will have been faced fairly and squarely. Along with doubting Thomas we shall genuinely be able to say, 'My Lord and my God', and thus to move forward. After all, a faith that, like the fairy tales and Father Christmas, is based on 'a willing suspension of disbelief' is really not worth holding on to. Either it has got to get stronger and more real, or you might as well give it up!

It was not until I was able to say to Him, 'Lord, I believe, help my unbelief,' that God could move in to help me from the *real* situation, rather than the somewhat shaky front-room position that I had somehow managed to maintain up to that point.

In fact someone showed me the promise in Luke, Chapter 11, verse 13, where it says, 'If you then, though you are evil, know how to give good gifts to your children, how much more will your Father in heaven give the Holy Spirit to those who ask him!'

The wonderful realisation that it was possible to *actually experience* the love and the power of God for *myself*, and that He really did care about *me personally*, despite all my failings, proved to be the door to abundant life that I had been looking for ever since I became a Christian several years previously. *But I had to ask a friend openly for directions first, thus admitting to the fact that I needed help*. And maybe this is our problem ...

As I have loved you so you must love one another

A key failing in our Anglo-Saxon brand of Christianity is that we like to keep our faith private between ourselves and God. To share or talk about this with others can often seem rather too embarrassing and difficult.

In the upper room on that final Friday night of His life Jesus left His disciples with the 'new commandment' ringing in their ears. When they loved one another, as He had loved them, then all men would know that they were His disciples. And if we are honest we must admit that there is no room left for an individualistic 'ivory-tower' relationship contained in these words – however much we would like there to be.

Love like this is all about making one another feel of value, and about being prepared to stay alongside our friends and neighbours through the good times and the bad, and during all those painful cellar experiences that they may be going through. In an ideal world, and maybe for some people reading this book, the love that I am speaking about may already be a normal part of everyday life, perhaps first experienced naturally and openly in the family home. In such a situation the love of God will simply be a wonderful enrichment. But we have to remember that it is *not* like this for *everyone*. I am constantly taken aback by some of the hurts and rejections that lie behind some of the very 'strong' and 'okay' masks that people unconsciously wear.

But when we have been truly released to find our own God-given identity through the real-life experience of His love and of others in His name, then we will be able to go out freely into the world, *genuinely* loving our neighbours as ourselves without fear of rejection.

To help others also

It is only when we have been willing to be vulnerable to one another in genuine sharing love and to look at the things that cause us pain, that we have the right to come alongside others in this way. Until we have received help with our *own* cellar areas, there is no way we can really go out to help other people, or to 'sit where they sit'.

When I first started on a counselling course, I imagined that this would give me the necessary 'knowledge' to help people in need. What I did *not* recognise at all was my *own* need of help, and the very crucial part that *this* would play in any future ministry.

As I had been helped myself, both by the genuine love of other Christian friends, and in counselling and inner healing, so I was able to help others also. At times it was almost uncanny how the help I received on one day would be exactly what was required for someone else on the next. In the end I found myself saying, 'Well, what do you want me to do with it this time, Lord?'

We are all sinners and we all have needs and problems, however good we may be at disguising them. For people in leadership positions it will probably be extra hard to admit this. They may need help to understand that God does not expect them to remain balanced on some kind of perfect pedestal, administering help to all comers, but never receiving it themselves.

Some people in leadership roles actually prefer the

pedestal situation. If you like it is an easy (though probably quite unconscious) defence against being vulnerable. Childhood hurts will have convinced these people early in life that unless they remain 'in control' of the situation (the group, the church, etc.) all will be lost. They may therefore need a great deal of loving sympathetic support before they will ever risk opening up to receive the help that others may well be longing to give them.

Freedom to be myself in communication

One area in which I found a really new freedom was that of communication. Not just as a writer and journalist, but also in being honestly myself with other people that I encountered in my everyday life.

Hitherto I had always felt under an obligation to quickly say something 'Christian' when meeting someone new. I found it very difficult just to be with people, listening to them and sitting where they sat. As a result my whole mind was much more preoccupied with what I was going to say than it was with genuine interest in them as people. This was so obviously a 'duty' exercise that listeners would pick it up in a flash. 'You only want to convert me – no thanks!' To be honest I see this syndrome at work in Christian circles time and again, and I believe it is almost more counter-productive than anything.

For my own part, since I have felt free to relax with people, I am constantly astonished at how many of them will *ask me* about my faith, and seem to want what I have – rather than my having to push this at them.

Recently someone paid me what I can only describe as a rather back-handed compliment, but it had quite frightening implications. I had only met her a couple of times very briefly on the tennis court, and she had subsequently discovered that I took part in a so-called 'religious' television programme. Her spontaneous reaction to a mutual friend was this – 'Ann Warren! But I thought she was such a normal kind of person.' Her previous experience of Christianity had been such that she *simply could not put together in the same category* someone who lived a *normal* relaxed kind of life, with someone who *also* took their faith seriously!

As with that frightening story that Murray Watts told, the world's image of anything involved with religion and Christianity is tainted, *not* with the real spontaneous life of God overflowing from the full hearts of His people, but by the sadly unnatural behaviour of so many of His followers who have never really learnt to be themselves.

It seems to me that God has little use for person-shaped tape recorders reeling off a pre-recorded message, but He *does* need living lights that shine out the reality of His love for them with words that flow spontaneously from a full heart.

Finders not keepers

While the criticism frequently levelled at those who want to find themselves is that they are 'self centred', I hope by now that I have finally disproved this argument.

It is only *when* we have truly found ourselves and our real value that the self-centred behaviour patterns and paralysing self consciousness can be completely cleared away, thus leaving the road clear for the love of God to come freely in. Then and only then will we be free to go out to others with the love that we have been given, truly forgetting about ourselves.

Our gratitude for all that God has done for us, and for the love that we have received, will be real because we have actually experienced this for ourselves. We will now be free to give as we have received.

However, I think it must be said that there are certain people who, having 'found themselves', will, initially at any rate, be reluctant to part with what they have so recently acquired. It is rather like a pendulum that swings too far the other way before it returns to centre.

All his life Richard had been at the beck and call of a very demanding mother, and he had carried this behaviour pattern on into his Christian life, almost enthusiastically submerging himself in the needs of others, while deep down resenting the demands that he imagined that others were making of him – but which he was actually imposing on himself. For several months after he found freedom, he went into what one can only describe as reverse gear, wanting to clasp all his newly found time and abilities to himself. In actual fact it was rather like a reliving of the proper childhood he had never had. But eventually he needed a push out into the world again in order to give love as he had received it. Without this in any case the happiness wells would have dried up. On the Dead Sea principle, it is necessary to give out to others the rivers of living water that God is busy pouring in, or the water will become stagnant and of no use anyway.

In my own case the syndrome was slightly different. When I had worked through the unhappiness of my childhood, I suddenly came out into a light and sunlit place where I realised the kind of person I would have been if it had not been for all that had happened to me ... The temptation again was to grab life for myself, and leave God out of my thinking – after all why had He allowed all this to happen to me in the first place?

It took only a couple of months to discover that life without God is a pretty pointless affair anyway, however much you are enjoying yourself! And when I came back to Him, this experience was yet another aid to 'sitting where they sit' outside the love and fellowship of the church.

Change can be frightening for others

During such journeys in search of our own identity, some pretty radical changes may be taking place – generally speaking, the more we have been through, the more dramatic they will be.

During this time, for instance, relationships with parents or spouses, not to mention close friends, will often reach a sudden and unexpected low, making people around us fear what is happening to us. Suddenly we seem to have become selfish and difficult as never before – particularly if we have tended to display only a smiling and compliant 'front-room' image previously. But this is an essential part of letting the real feelings out of our cellar area, so that they can freely become part of our normal identity – and to begin with there will probably be a fair degree of over-reaction.

Going back to my earlier diagram, the characteristics that make up 'who I am' may have to push their way fairly violently out of the walls that have confined them for so long in order to find release at all – and this often results in some pretty self-centred behaviour for a while.

But of course this must not remain so, and when the pendulum has swung back from this self-centred extreme, it will be with a much greater degree of wholeness. This will be no 'front-room' Christianity, but a well-lit house that the love of God can move through freely, reaching out without fear to those around us.

> I said to the man who stood at the gate of the year, 'Give me a lantern that I may tread safely into the unknown.' And he replied, 'Go out into the darkness and put thine hand into the hand of God. That shall be to thee better than light and safer than a known way.'

Like most journeys that we undertake with God as our guide, this one is unlikely to be plain sailing, and there will be many around us who want us to stay as we are, safely going through the motions of our faith. But it seems to me that the choice before us is a fairly clear one. If we do not know that we are really loved or of value in God's eyes, then we can either carry on as before, without experiencing a great deal of love, joy or peace, or else we can set out on the voyage of self discovery with God as our pilot, launching out into the deep uncharted waters of the river of life.

> Swarms of living creatures will live wherever the river flows. There will be large numbers of fish, because this water flows there and makes the salt water fresh; so where the river flows everything will live ... Fruit trees of all kinds will grow on both banks of the river. Their leaves will not wither nor will their fruit fail. Every month they will bear, because the water from the sanctuary flows to them. Their fruit will serve for food and their leaves for healing. (Ezekiel 47: 9, 12 N.V.)

More than anything I believe that almighty God longs to bring us into the mainstream flow of this river, experiencing the full joy and strength of His power and love. But first He may have to remove the blocks that hinder its flow and dam up the water from reaching us in anything more than a pathetic trickle. Above all He does not want us to go out empty-handed into a world that desperately needs this water of life. If we cannot consider our *own* needs, then at least we must see how the blocks in our lives are hindering the love of God from reaching out to those around us.

Perhaps it will appear that there is no one around who will understand or have enough loving concern to listen. Or maybe we have even experienced hurtful rejections if we have ever tried to talk about this. Certainly it is of the highest priority that those who help in the name of Christ should not be guilty of letting us down again – although we are all human and fallible and there is no way that this can be avoided altogether.

Certainly all I can say from my own experience is that there is no way that anyone could drag me back screaming into the time before I allowed God to come in and clear out the cellars of my life. My defences were very strong, and it took a lot of loving patience for others to get through, but the freedom from the chains of the past that had bound me was the most wonderful release imaginable.

What kind of person am I? Does God *really* love me? What are the gifts that He has given to me especially, and what does He want me to do with them? What do I do with all the hurts and fears that haunt my dreams, and fill my mind when I am trying to pray and think of others? How can *anyone* love the real me?

Until these and many other such questions have been answered for us, we shall never be free to know the wonder of His love, or the inner certainty of a faith that is based on solid cellar foundations, nothing hidden away beneath the cobwebs. But when we have faced up to all this, trusting God and our fellow Christians to give us the loving support that we so badly need, abundant life then becomes a reality and not just an impossible dream.

Useful Addresses

Care and Counsel
146 Queen Victoria St
London EC4V 4BX
(01 236 4970)

is an evangelical Christian organisation staffed by professionally qualified therapists all of whom are practising Christians. They provide individual and group therapy, as well as arranging public conferences and short teaching courses.

**Clinical Theology
  Association**
St Mary's House
Church Westcote
Oxford OX7 6SF
(0993 830209)

 trains ordained and lay people in Christian pastoral care and aims to deepen Christian life and growth towards personal maturity and stability. It provides workshops, growth groups, and a two-year course of twenty-four three-hour seminars in human relations, pastoral care and counselling in many different parts of the country. Individual counselling help is also available.

**CWR Institute in
  Christian Counselling**
Portman House
Colby Road

aims to present a working biblical approach to the solving of human problems. They have just started a

Walton on Thames
Surrey KT12 2RN
(0932 245202)

regional counsellor training scheme in response to many requests from ministers and church leaders throughout the country. The training programme is under the leadership of Selwyn Hughes and Trevor Partridge.

Westminster Pastoral
   Foundation
23 Kensington Square
London W8 5HN
(01 937 6956)

This provides a Christian-based counselling service and training agency for counsellors, and a number of affiliated services nationwide.

Wholeness in Christ
Central Coordinator
29 Churchfield Road
Houghton Regis
Beds LU5 5HL

is one of the ministries of the Holy Spirit to the whole person, practised by Christians to Christians. They organise retreats, schools of prayer counselling and parish weekends run by their own team of counsellors.

This is by no means a comprehensive list of counselling centres in the UK, but it represents those either known to me personally or recommended by people whose judgement I trust.

Inevitably, as with ministers and doctors, not every counsellor will suit every individual. Similarly, differing approaches to the Christian faith will mean that people will need to look for help where they feel most at home. Some organisations use the primarily psychological approach from a Christian-based standpoint, others take a more straightforward biblical approach and expect to use the gifts of the Spirit. As I said in the book it is important to keep looking until we find the help and healing we need.

Many different denominations have now started counselling centres, and as a starting point it may be helpful to ask your own minister what help is available in your immediate area.